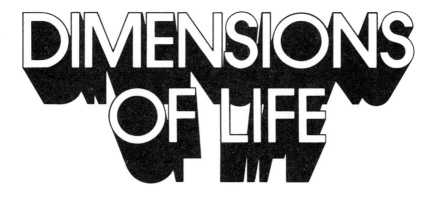

Paul H. Dunn
Maurine Ward

Bookcraft
Salt Lake City, Utah

Library of Congress Catalog Card Number: 79-52231
ISBN O-88494-375-5

2nd Printing, 1979

Lithographed in the United States of America
PUBLISHERS PRESS
Salt Lake City, Utah

PREFACE

Life has many dimensions. It is full of challenges and joys. The abundant life can best be achieved through the practical application of true gospel principles.

This volume attempts to assist the reader in discovering new ways in broadening life's dimensions.

I am very grateful to Maurine Ward for her assistance and great writing talent. Her own life is a marvelous example of the truths contained here.

Thanks to my good friend, David Christensen, for his insights and ideas.

A special thanks to Sharene Miner Hansen, my secretary, for her devoted work and skills.

I am always grateful to my wife, Jeanne, for her encouragement and sustaining influence. As usual her insights and gentle touch are found in every chapter.

I particularly appreciate the love and support of my daughters, Janet, Marsha, and Kellie, and their husbands and children.

— PAUL H. DUNN

CONTENTS

PART ONE

THE GAUGE
OF GROWTH

THE POWER OF THE SELF-FULFILLING PROPHECY

The Duke of Wellington once said that the reason the British army won the Battle of Waterloo was not because the British soldiers were braver than the French soldiers, but simply because they were brave five minutes longer." (William K. Reid, Sr., *Moral, Ethical and Inspirational Readings* [J. Weston Walch], p. 8.)

Isn't that the case in life? The margin between winning and losing — between first and second place — is often a very small one. The last five minutes, the last second, the last out, the last push when a push seemed impossible is usually the difference between defeat and victory. Many men and women have gone down to defeat, have watched their dearest dreams wash away, simply because they gave up five minutes too soon.

As I've pondered this great truth, I've wondered what it was that gave life's winners in every field the courage and stamina to give that last push to victory. Where did they find the strength to see them through that last five minutes when the rest of us floundered and failed? And I've come to believe this: the winner always knew he would be a winner. Somebody convinced him that he could do it.

Somebody believed in him and made him believe in himself. This great principle is called self-fulfilling prophecy, and it has the power to change each of us.

What is a self-fulfilling prophecy? It is the tendency of certain kinds of predictions to bring about the conditions that make them come true. Estimating the most advantageous time to plant can never change a growing season or prevent a late frost, but advertising a product as extremely popular will frequently make it so. Similarly, predicting the success of a student, an athlete, or a worker by expressing faith in him can affect his capacity for achievement. Some things in life we cannot forecast; but people, whether in groups or individually, tend to meet our expectations for them.

Think of self-fulfilling prophecies in your own life. You perform better for some people than you do for others, because you know they believe in you. You do the things in life you think you can, that you've been told you can. Consider this. If someone asked you to walk a foot-wide, ten-foot plank across the floor without falling off, you'd do it in a second. You know you can. There's nothing hard about that. But if that foot-wide, ten-foot plank was raised one hundred feet above the ground and poised between two buildings, not many of us would volunteer to walk it. Why? The plank really isn't any different. The only thing that has changed is our belief that we can walk across the plank with ease. The plank is the same, but our belief in ourselves is different. The belief that we are big enough to do the job — any job — often makes the difference between whether we can do it or not.

Harvard psychologist Robert Rosenthal was interested in the power of the self-fulfilling prophecy. He wanted to see if teachers' predictions of student ability could actually be a factor in raising I.Q. scores of schoolchildren.

In a preliminary test Rosenthal gave each of twelve psychology students five rats of the same strain. Half of these students were told that their rats were specially bred to be excellent at running a maze. The second group of students was told that, for genetic reasons, their rats could be expected to be poor at running a maze.

Throughout the entire experiment the rats whose handlers believed they had special potential did, in fact, run the maze better; the rats whose trainers expected them to be slow performed poorly, and sometimes refused to run at all. Yet the only difference between the two sets of rats was the attitudes of their trainers.

How did one group of rats know that more was expected of them? Rosenthal says, "The students with the [so-called] 'bright' rats gave their animals more attention and handled them more gently than did the students expecting poor performance." (John Kord Lagemann, "Self-Fulfilling Prophecy — A Key to Success," *Reader's Digest*, February 1969, p. 81.)

Rosenthal was then ready to try his experiment on schoolchildren and their teachers. Children from kindergarten through fifth grade in one school were given what was called a new test of learning ability to determine which students were exceptionally gifted. The teachers were then informed that certain designated children in their classes were especially bright. This, of course, was not true: the children had been picked on a completely random basis, and their "gifts" were only in the minds of the teachers.

But by the end of the year there was indeed a difference in those children who had been designated as bright. Their I.Q.s had soared ahead of those of the other children, increasing by as many as fifteen to twenty-seven I.Q. points.

The explanation? Rosenthal said: "It probably lies in the subtle interaction between teacher and pupils. Tone of voice, facial expressions, touch and posture may be the means by which — often unwittingly — she communicates her expectations to her pupils. Such communication may help a child by changing his perceptions of himself." (Lagemann, p. 81.)

When it comes right down to it, our perceptions of ourselves may be the most important factor in determining the quality of our lives. If we believe we are defeated nobodies, that perception chokes off all our abilities. They simply wither away. But if we believe we can do it, that we were built for success, then we have the staying power to give that extra push. And most often we believe in ourselves because somebody else believed in us first.

When a trainer believes in an athlete, the athlete can't let that trainer down. When a parent believes in a child, the child when tempted says, "I can't; my father trusts me." When a teacher believes in the abilities of a ghetto child, the child defies environment to become a great statesman. The examples abound. The prophecies become self-fulfilling. The author of Proverbs taught, "As [a man] thinketh in his heart, so is he." (Proverbs 23:7.)

Each of us needs to employ that power of the self-fulfilling prophecy to motivate our own husbands, our wives, and our children to their highest potential. Think of what could be accomplished. If we enlarge our mental picture of them, they will grow to fit that idea. It's just too easy to pigeonhole those around us. There's the clown of the family, the smart one, the athlete. And those children grow up to be just what we thought they were. Most of us aren't much better with our mates. We say, "I knew you'd do that," or, "You always do this." And we aren't surprised when they live up — or down — to our expectations.

Fortify your family for the battles of life by believing in them and in their vast potential. Arm them with the knowledge that you know they will never let you down, that they are winners, and that against any odds they have someone who believes in them. They'll become who you think they are. And when it takes five more minutes of being brave or one last push to win the race, they'll find that stamina in your self-fulfilling prophecy, in your love.

MAN'S GREATEST NEED

One day in Ancient Greece, the citizens of the community awoke to a small disaster. The sacred statue of their god Zeus that stood in the public square had been vandalized. This was a crime of the worst kind, and a public frenzy immediately arose. "Catch the offender!" came the outcry, but days went by and the villain was not caught.

Some weeks later, the citizens awoke to find another of their sacred statues desecrated. They were furious at whoever would dare to do such a thing, and they determined to go to any length to catch him. Appropriately, guards were appointed to stand watch over the sacred monuments around the clock until the guilty party was caught.

At last, when he attempted a third vandalous act, the guilty man was captured and was taken before the tribunal of the people.

"Do you realize what you have done?" the officials asked the guilty man.

"Yes, I do," he said.

"Do you realize the penalty for your crime?"

"Death," the man answered, almost merrily.

The officials then asked, "You understood the severe penalty which accompanied your crime and yet you dared to do such a thing. Why?"

The man answered in a steady voice. "My whole life I've been a nobody," he said. "I knew I would always be a nobody, that I would never be worthy of the least bit of attention from my comrades. I'm not a nobody anymore. Now I'm a somebody. Everyone will know who I am and remember me. Death is a small price to pay for immortality." (Adapted from Lajos Egri, *The Art of Dramatic Writing* [New York: Simon and Schuster, 1946].)

While that man's act is unique, his need is universal. *Everybody wants to be a somebody.* In fact, next to food, warmth, and shelter, the need to be important is the deepest urge in human nature. When people don't feel like they matter, dire consequences result. A feeling of worthlessness is the root of almost all antisocial behavior — vandalism, low achievement, hostility. The list goes on and on. Have you ever read Jean E. Mizer's story of "The Cipher in the Snow"? It tells of a young boy who struggled to the front of his school bus and asked the driver to stop; the driver stopped, and the boy swayed down the steps of the bus and fell face first in the snow — dead. The school children, the school administrators, the teachers, and the members of the community were horrified, especially when they received the medical report on the boy's death. No apparent cause of death could be found.

The boy's former math teacher, a man who could only vaguely remember him from the year before, decided to look further into the case. He inquired around school, trying to learn more about the boy, and he found out that no one knew anything about him. The boy had gone to school in the community for eight years and no one remembered him, no one had called him friend. The girl who had sat next to him in math class didn't even know what he had looked like. Many were not even aware that he existed. As far as most were concerned, the boy was a zero, and the boy knew it. The teacher eventually realized that the boy could finally take no more. The boy had just given up and died. (Stan and Sharon Miller, *Especially for Mormons,* vol. 1 [Provo, Utah: Kellirae Arts, 1971], pp. 352-54.)

These feelings are not confined only to the small or the weak or the insignificant. Lord Chesterfield himself said, "I would rather be in company with a dead man than with an absent one; for if the dead man gives me no pleasure, at least he shows me no contempt; whereas the absent man, silently indeed, but very plainly, tells me that he does not think me worth his attention." (Richard L. Evans, *Richard Evans' Quote Book* [Salt Lake City: Publishers Press, 1971]; p. 172.)

Since everybody has such a profound need to be a somebody, surely the greatest gift we can give another is the sense of his own importance. We have that terrible and wonderful power to build another person or to ignore him and perhaps shatter him with our indifference. The sad thing is that those who most need to be reassured of their *worth* may be the very ones we are even *now* automatically dismissing as not *worthy* of such an effort on our part.

Let us be the ones who protect and enlarge the self-respect of the people we meet. Let us be the ones to see beyond the surface, however rough, into the feelings of those we meet each day. It takes a special empathy, a gracious heart to build the ego of another person. It may be done with a single word, a look, a gesture; but there are very few who have ever understood, let alone mastered, this gentle art. Remember:

> Within the oyster shell uncouth
> the purest pearl may hide,
> And oft you'll find a heart of truth,
> within a rough outside.

Elizabeth Byrd, a writer of historical novels, tells a story about how she came to sense this special gift in another. She was on the way to Inverness, Scotland, when she struck up a conversation with a big, rawboned farm woman sitting next to her on the bus. The woman asked her to come home to spend the evening with her since her husband had gone off to market. By the time Miss Byrd and the farm woman arrived at the cottage, a bleak building on a lonely slope, it was raining hard. They hadn't been there long when suddenly the lights flickered and died. Mrs. McIntosh, the farm woman, sighed, "The power's out," and she lit candles to cast some light on the room. While she was making a fire there was a knock on the door.

She opened it and a young boy came in. She took his dripping coat and cap, and as he moved into the firelight Miss Byrd saw that he was about twelve years old — and pitifully crippled.

After he caught his breath, he said: "My father tried to ring you, but your phone is dead. I came to see that you're all right."

"Thank you, John," she said. The wind rose, raving and screaming, battering the shutters.

"You're not scared?" the crippled boy asked Miss Byrd.

Miss Byrd started to say no, but Mrs. McIntosh, though obviously unafraid, quickly said what the boy wanted to hear: "Of course she was scared, and so was I. But now we've got a *man* about."

There was a moment's silence. Then he arose. "I'll see that everything's snug," he said. And he hobbled slowly out of the room, a slight swagger to his step.

Elizabeth Byrd asked herself for weeks afterwards why she hadn't answered the boy's question as had Mrs. McIntosh. Mrs. McIntosh had given the boy a sense of self-worth. How often before in her life, she wondered, had she failed to recognize another's need? By what magic had Mrs. McIntosh transformed a crippled boy into a confident man? (Paraphrased from Stan and Sharon Miller, *Especially for Mormons,* vol. 3 [Provo, Utah: Kellirae Arts, 1976], pp. 176-77.)

For the benefit and blessing of us all, we all need desperately to learn this compassion, this tact, this sensitivity so that we can build the lives of others. It may be as simple an act as remembering the name of someone you've met only once or asking the social wallflower to dance; it may be giving your wife a special gift that makes her feel beautiful or giving a word of praise to someone hungering for it. Do you notice the child without a friend, the neighbor left out of a party?

"When you come home from work and your child races to greet you, asking excitedly, 'Did you hear what happened on Main Street today?' your gracious heart, somehow, has not heard the news — it gives the child the pleasure of telling you. But if you say, 'Oh, yes I heard about it an hour ago,' " think of the consequences. (Stan and Sharon Miller, vol. 3, p. 178.)

Do you yearn to be a somebody? We all do. Remember that. Make another person feel like a somebody, and you're halfway to being there yourself.

HELP WHEN IT HURTS

As we make our way along this dangerous mortal journey, the greatest comfort of all is to feel that our hand is in the Lord's; that he'll comfort us as we face life's many hazards; that somehow, just by asking, all our wishes will come true. Yet surely one of life's most sobering lessons is to find that we don't always get what we ask for — even from a loving Father in heaven. We may ask for something righteous, necessary, or even important to us and it may not come to pass. Who can explain it?

Look at the evidence. Two beautiful women are with child, counting the days until a perfect human being is born into the world; each is praying for the safety of the new life she carries near her heart. The day of delivery comes for each of them. One bears a healthy, bright-eyed baby; the other, a child blind and deaf, a child who will never be able to hear symphonies or gaze at blue skies. Our angry hearts cry out for justice. How can the Lord allow such pain?

Look at still more evidence. Dr. Truman Madsen, a philosophy professor, sat with his family watching the movie, *The Greatest Story Ever Told*. At one point the family saw "a sinister Herod send his soldiers to Bethlehem. Then come the screams of mothers, glimpses of blood-smirched swords pulled from children's bodies. Then you see Mary and Joseph who have received Divine warning, walking peacefully with their Babe toward the safety of Egypt." As the scene closed, Dr. Madsen's little girl grabbed his hand and whispered in confusion and fright, "Daddy, didn't Heavenly Father care about those other children?" (Truman Madsen, *Four Essays on Love* [Salt Lake City: Bookcraft, Inc., 1977], pp. 55-56.)

We wonder if the Lord cares about *us* as we plead on bended knee for the Lord to save the life of our husband or father or sweetheart or child, and the heavens answer with the stillness of death. We wonder if the Lord cares about *them* as we walk through a hospital ward and see patients wracked with pain in a struggle with cancer, or as we walk down ghetto streets and see children who are abused or hungry.

Indeed, the critics of Christianity point to the world and tell us that the history of this globe is nothing but crime, pestilence, war, and terror. They ask how we can say there is an all-wise, all-good Father in heaven who cares what happens here.

All this supposes that God both can and should prevent misfortunes from happening to us. That idea deserves a second look.

Let's talk first about what God can do. Those who are bitter because God has not miraculously stopped their painful experiences, has not whisked away their private tragedies, consider this: we live in a world where the laws of nature are fixed and stable. As one writer said: "The permanent nature of wood which enables us to use it as a beam also enables us to use it for hitting our neighbor on the head. The permanent nature of matter in general means that when human beings fight, the victory ordinarily goes to those who have superior weapons, skill, and numbers, even if their cause is unjust.

"We can, perhaps, conceive of a world in which God corrected the results of this abuse of free-will by His creatures at every moment: so that a wooden beam became soft as grass when it was used as a weapon, and the air refused to obey me if I attempted to set up in it the sound waves that carry lies or insults. But such a world would be one in which wrong actions were impossible, and in which, therefore, freedom of the will would be void. . . . All matter in the neighbourhood of a wicked man would be liable to undergo unpredictable alterations." (C. S. Lewis, *The Problem of Pain* [London: Fontana Books, 1957], p. 21.)

This is not to say that the Lord doesn't sometimes work miracles that work through the laws we don't understand, but basically our environment as we know it is stable and unchanging, an environment we can count on.

Now let's look at the other question. Shouldn't God prevent our misfortunes? Shouldn't he grant all our wishes so that our lives are as easy as a summer vacation?

My answer to that is a simple *no.* God's goal for us is not just that it might be said of this earth experience that a good time was had by all. His love for us is made of sterner stuff than that. He cannot give us everything we ask for, or help us sidestep all suffering; the result would be fragile souls unable to endure. We are God's children, and like any loving parent he cannot be satisfied with us until we have a certain character, a certain nobility. Mortality has purpose. We are here to learn how to be like him, and free agency is the key.

Just as necessity is the mother of invention, so is adversity the parent of all character development.

Maltbie Babcock wrote: "Present suffering is not enjoyable, but life would be worth little without it. The difference between iron and steel is fire, but steel is worth all it costs. Iron ore may think itself senselessly tortured in the furnace, but when the watchspring looks back, it knows better."

At the age of seventeen a Nova Scotia farm boy named Alfred Fuller went to Boston, where he got a job selling brushes. He failed miserably at it. That failure was to be the turning point of his life. While he went on to do other jobs, working as a streetcar conductor and as a delivery boy, he kept asking why he had failed as a brush salesman.

He finally decided that the failure had not been his, but that of the brushes. They were not designed to fit the needs of the average housewife. To vindicate himself, he took his meager savings, bought a used wire-twisting machine, wire, and bristles, and began making brushes that he thought would sell. They did. At first he had to make the brushes and sell them himself. Today he has several thousand employees and many thousands of salesmen. Fuller brushes are a national institution that represent a multimillion-dollar business because a boy of seventeen met misfortune and literally twisted that failure into success.

In the town of Enterprise, Alabama, there is a monument in

honor of the boll weevil. Knowing that this dreaded insect pest of the cotton country once threatened to ruin this important crop, one wonders why anyone would erect a monument to it. But it seems that inroads of the boll weevil and its destruction of thousands of acres of cotton crops resulted in the planting of other crops — such as the sweet potato and the peanut — which brought a more stable and prosperous economy to the South. In other words, the enemy boll weevil did the South a good turn. The bad break became a good one.

Louise Lake, a lovely woman and personal friend who is confined to a wheelchair, made this insightful comment: "How can one learn to endure, if he has nothing to endure?"

Still, it hurts not to get what we ask for in prayer. It hurts to suffer when it seems the Lord could take our burdens away. Pain that later turns to good fortune, pain that refines our character, is still, after all, pain.

Where is our consolation?

The Lord gave a modern prophet three keys to help him understand and endure affliction. First he said, "My son, peace be unto thy soul; thine adversity and thine afflictions shall be but a small moment." (D&C 121:7.) No matter how sore our tragedy, how unbearable our ache, it will eventually come to an end and be but a memory.

Second, the Lord told this prophet, "Thou art not yet as Job." (D&C 121:10.) No matter how bad our lot is in life, we have innumerable blessings. A Persian legend relates, "I complained that I had not shoes until I saw a man who had not feet."

Finally, the Lord said to this prophet, "And if thou be cast into the pit, or into the hands of murderers, and the sentence of death passed upon thee; if thou be cast into the deep; if the billowing surge conspire against thee; if fierce winds become thine enemy; if the heavens gather blackness, and all the elements combine to hedge up the way; and above all, if the very jaws of hell shall gape open the mouth wide after thee, know thou, my son, that all these things give thee experience, and shall be for thy good.

"The Son of Man hath descended below them all. Art thou greater than he?" (D&C 122:7-8.)

As was the case with Joseph Smith, so it is with us. If we endure the pains of life well, even those times when the heavens seem to turn a deaf ear on us, our God will exalt us on high, and we will triumph over all our foes.

RAISED BY A POWER OF ONE

You can always tell when it's back-to-school time. You can see it in newspaper ads advertising the latest in school fashions. You can see it on drugstore shelves loaded with notebooks, pencils, and pens. But most of all you can see it in the faces of students who are just realizing that the wonderful endless summer really has an end.

For those who are headed back to the ivied halls of learning, take heart that your schools aren't like the early ones in America's history. One person of those times wrote that the schools "contain cold winds whistling in through cracks in the walls and breaks in the windows, volumes of smoke belching out from broken chimneys, and stifling air and nauseating smell ... such as a grown man has hardly been compelled to live in since the time of Jonah." Doesn't sound very inviting, does it?

But worse than the structural inadequacies in the early American schools was the punishment meted out to the truant. The *Boston Transcript* reported in the early nineteenth century that one delicate boy was made to kneel over a desk and was given ninety blows with a large instrument at intervals over three hours, resulting in a temporary loss of his ability to walk. I'll bet he thought twice before missing school again.

I remember vividly my own school experience, sitting in those long English classes dreaming about becoming a member of the Hall of Fame while I couldn't even figure out what a dangling participle was.

I think most of us are a little like I was. We all want to be a somebody. As we grow up we have in our mind's eye visions of ourselves receiving a Nobel Prize, being written up on the cover of the latest national magazine, or standing in the spotlight and hearing the applause of our fans. At some time in our lives, most of us have believed we were meant to excel, to be someone special. But then something happens. A different attitude takes over. Our thinking shifts, and we begin to say to ourselves, "Oh, well, what can one person do anyway?" We begin to lose direction.

The great Cunard shipping line of Great Britain has built some of the most magnificent ships in history, but one was extraordinary. Commissioned by the government to build a great military vessel, the shipbuilders constructed one that seemed to be engineered perfectly. Every detail was precise; every piece of equipment was the best available. But one little thing was wrong with the ship. Its great propeller was just slightly crooked — not really enough so anyone could notice, but just slightly askew. And when they took that great ship out for its maiden voyage, the builders discovered something terrible. The ship could not be steered in a straight line. It just went around in circles because of its slightly crooked propeller. Because this fine ship had no direction, it had to be scrapped and sold for razor blades.

I think a lot of us are like that ship. We lose sight of our goals. We forget the direction we are headed in, and we end up wasting our time going around in circles. We become no more use than scrap metal. School starts, and we don't give it our best efforts. We don't turn assignments in on time. We don't study the reading material. We don't listen and probe and question in class. A new job starts and we don't hit each day with enthusiasm. We don't want to put in the extra hours to excel. It's so easy to think, "What difference can I make anyway?"

Have you ever heard the fable about the villagers who each agreed to contribute a sack of grain for those of their neighborhood who were ill or poor?

A large vat was put in the village square where sacks of grain were to be emptied. The day appointed for the opening arrived, the villagers assembled, the vat cover was lifted. It was empty! Each villager, thinking his grain would not be missed, had failed to respond! (Richard Pitts, alumni letter, Chapman College, Orange, California.)

You, whoever you are, have a great contribution to make to this world if you are willing to prepare for it in school, in work, in your odd hours. You were meant to make a difference in this world.

"I am just one woman," said a fine young college girl.

Let me ask, with Gordon Owen, "How many women does she want to be? What more can she ever hope to be than what she is; one woman? What was Florence Nightingale but one woman? Yet her work led straight to the Red Cross! How far would be the humane processes of healing the wounded and sorrowful all over the world today had this English nurse sat down and bemoaned the fact that she was 'just one woman'? Nor did Florence Nightingale wait for others. When all the medical officers had retired for the night, dog-tired, and silence and darkness had settled upon those miles of prostrate sick, the light of a single little lamp could be seen moving from cot to cot in a solitary round. It was the lamp of Florence Nightingale. 'Just one woman!'

"Where would the marvellous work done by radium be today if, when bereaved, Madame Curie had folded her hands when her husband passed away and minimized herself by saying, 'I am just one woman'?

"Yes, but singularly gifted, you say, were these women. Not according to their own testimonies. Quite to the contrary. 'I had faith: that was all,' said Florence Nightingale. 'I had confidence, little else,' said Madame Curie, and to their work each applied her fullest aspiration and trust." (Gordon Owen, *Midnight Meditations* [Salt Lake City: Gordon Owen], p. 32.)

"I am just one man," says another person.

Just one man, you say. Benjamin Franklin was just one man when he donated 116 books to a small city in Massachusetts. (The town had asked for a bell, but, always practical, Franklin sent books instead with the note, "Sense is preferable to sound.") That may not sound like such a big thing, but do you know who became literate by reading those 116 books? Horace Mann.

And it was just one man — in this case, Horace Mann — who traveled around America lecturing until he jolted our thinking into providing free public schools for all citizens. Where would any of us be without his great idea?

What can just one person do? Change the history of the world; change the heart of another soul; touch lives in ways more profound that you can dream. But that one person won't be you unless you begin to prepare now for a life of excellence, unless you set personal standards that are unimpeachable, unless you give every day your all. It's never too late to start.

When your heart is failing and you must have surgery, who do you seek for your physician? Some average guy who barely made it through medical school? Or do you seek the best? When your fortune or reputation hangs in the balance and you are faced with a tricky lawsuit, who do you seek for advice? Someone who doesn't understand the appropriate legal code, who doesn't take his work seriously?

I'll never forget the dentist who, while performing a root canal, leaned over his patient's mouth and said, "Oh, by the way — I got a D+ on this procedure in dental school."

Whatever you choose to do, whatever you choose to be, beat your own best record. All mankind needs your contribution. It was Horace Mann, again, who said, "Be ashamed to die until you have won some victory for mankind."

Remember, it is the glory of God that is intelligence.

NOTHING GETS US DOWN

One man came from hearing a series of inspirational talks the other day and said this: "When I hear talks like that I believe I could do or be anything. It seems there is no limit to my potential, to my energy, to my will to succeed. And then on the way home I get a flat tire and have to change it in the rain. I arrive home to find that one child is sick, that the dishwasher is broken, and that I have received a letter from the IRS saying I owe an extra five hundred dollars. To top that, my daughter has spilled liquid bleach on the living room carpet. It just takes a few hours back in the real world to forget all I heard from those inspirational talks and to make me thoroughly deflated."

Does this man's plight sound familiar? It seems to most of us that we could cope heroically with any of the large issues. We could be courageous, dedicated, even noble if life's challenges would just attack us one at a time. We could do incredible things. But we fall apart as a result of all the pesky little irritations that constantly surround us. We let trivialities worry us, fragment us — yes, even beat us. Sometimes in the battle of life we would like to shout, "Uncle! You win! I've had it. I'm through."

When I feel like that I like to think of what a grandmother said to her small granddaughter who was crying about a little disappointment. "Darling," she said, "repeat this and believe it. I will not be beat. I will not give up. Nothing gets us down. C'mon," said the grandmother, "you say it. I will not be beat. I will not give up. Nothing gets us down." As that scene unfolded between the woman and her grandchild, I saw a little miracle. Gradually the child stopped crying, and she eventually listened and staightened up. Something strong grew within her soul. "I will not give up," she finally said. "Nothing gets us down."

When life's small furies come crashing in upon us and all we'd like to do is give up or retreat, we need to remember this message: he can who thinks he can. One of the outstanding examples of this principle is the remarkable story of Legson Kayira, a teenage boy who lived in a tiny African village. Here is the story in his own words:

"My mother did not know where America was. I said to her, 'Mother, I want to go to America to go to college. Will you give me your permission?'

" 'Very well,' she said. 'You may go. When will you leave?'

"I did not want to give her time to discover how far America was, for fear that she would change her mind. 'Tomorrow,' I said. . . .

"I left my home in northern Nyasaland, East Africa. I had only the clothes I wore, a khaki shirt and shorts. . . . I carried, too, the maize my mother had given me, wrapped in banana leaves.

"My goal was a continent and an ocean away, but I did not doubt that I would reach it. . . .

From the . . . [Christian] missionaries [who had passed through my village] I learned that I had an obligation to use whatever talents I had to make life better for others. And to do that I would need an education. . . .

"My intention was to make my way to Cairo . . . 3,000 miles away, a distance I could not comprehend, and I foolishly thought I could walk it in four or five days. But in four or five days I was only about 25 miles from home, my food was gone, I had no money, and I did not know what to do, except that I must keep going.

"I developed a pattern of travel that became my life for more than a year. Villages were usually five or six miles apart, on forest paths. I would arrive at one in the afternoon and ask if I could work to earn food, water, and a place to sleep. When this was possible, I would spend the night there, then move to the next village. . . . Malaria mosquitoes . . . were constant companions, and I often was sick.

"By the end of a year I had walked 1,000 miles and had arrived in Uganda, where a family took me in. . . .

"In Kampala, I unexpectedly came upon a directory of American colleges. Opening it at random, I saw the name of Skagit Valley College, Mount Vernon, Washington. I had heard that American colleges sometimes gave scholarships to deserving young people, so I wrote and applied for one. I realized that I might be refused but was not discouraged. I would write to one school after another in the directory until I found one that would help me.

"Three weeks later I was granted a scholarship and assured that the school would help me find a job. Overjoyed, I went to the United States authorities only to be told that this was not enough. I would need a passport and the round-trip fare in order to obtain a visa.

"I wrote to the government for a passport but it was refused because I could not tell them when I was born. I then wrote to the missionaries who had taught me in my childhood, and through their efforts was granted a passport. But I still could not get a visa because I did not have the fare.

"Still determined, I resumed my journey. So strong was my faith that I used my last money to buy my first pair of shoes: I knew I could not walk into college in my bare feet. I carried the shoes to save them.

"Across Uganda and into the Sudan I walked. The villages were farther apart and the people were less friendly. Sometimes I had to walk 20 or 30 miles in a day to find a place to sleep or to work to earn some food. At last I reached Khartoum, where I learned that there was a United States consulate. . . .

"The Consul was interested enough to write the college in America about my plight. Back came a cable.

"The students, hearing about me and my problems, had raised the fare of $1,700. . . ."

In his speech of gratitude to the student body he said: "When God has put an impossible dream in your heart, He means to help you fulfill it. I believed this to be true when, as an African bush boy, I felt compelled to become an American college graduate."*

---

*"Barefoot to America," by Legson Kayira, from GUIDEPOSTS TREASURY OF FAITH. Copyright © 1970 by the Guidepost Associates, Inc. Reprinted by permission of Doubleday and Company, Inc.

To update the story, you should know that Mr. Kayira became a professor of political science at Cambridge University in England. He authored a novel, and a nonfiction book based on African life.

Do you ever feel like giving up? We all do, but we must tell ourselves again and again that nothing will get us down. All the great things that were ever done in this world were accomplished by people who refused to give up. Someone has to do everything. Someone has to write the books, discover scientific secrets, lead governments. Someone has to learn, to work, to plan, to risk, to believe. And nobody really has it any easier than you do.

We must be counted with Legson, who walked twenty-five hundred miles to fulfill a dream. We must be counted with Admiral Peary who, when he was disabled with the agony of frozen feet that threatened to defeat his heroic effort to reach the North Pole, wrote this on the wall of his miserable shelter: "I shall find a way or make one." (Richard L. Evans, *An Open Road: Volume III of Thoughts for One Hundred Days* [Salt Lake City: Publishers Press, 1968], p. 176.)

May we all join the ranks of those who have learned to never give up.

WHAT'S YOUR EXCUSE?

What's your excuse for not being who you were meant to be, for not living up to that idealized picture of yourself you carry in your head? Most of us have a sweet vision of ourselves as someone better; that vision will never come about until we master our appetites, lose a few pounds, work when we'd rather play, carry on undaunted in the face of disappointment. But let's face it. When it comes right down to living up to our standards, we can find a million excuses not to. What's yours?

I know a person who's never on time. It's a habit that exasperates her far more than it does her friends, who are often waiting five or ten minutes for her arrival. But she has a different, maybe even a valid, excuse each time she walks out the door a few minutes late. "I was all ready, but the phone rang." "I forgot something and had to go back." "I just couldn't get my children moving," she says to rationalize her tardiness. But in reality the only one she's fooling is herself. Because her personal standard is timeliness, she honestly believes she is basically a timely person. She can't see that she has rationalized herself well away from that standard with a series of weak excuses.

You see multiples of this example wherever you turn. "I'm basically a loving person," says one of us, "But I'm just too busy to get involved this time." "I'm basically overweight," says another, "and I'll start my diet after this party, or maybe I'll start it tomorrow." "I'm a great parent," says still another, "and I'll read to my children next week when this project is finished."

It is remarkably easy for all of us to break our own rules, trample on our standards, and excuse ourselves by thinking: "I'm OK. I know better. It's just for this time. There's always tomorrow. They'll understand."

But as St. Augustine said, "For it is one thing to see the land of peace from a wooded ridge . . . and another to tread the road that leads to it." And I add, it is one thing to know what we must do to be our idealized person, and it is another thing to be there.

Maybe it is this duality, this sense of knowing our standards and identifying with them but finding excuses to never quite meet them, that led to this observation by Tom Knight: "Isn't it funny that when the other fellow takes a long time to do something, he's slow. When I take a long time to do something, I'm thorough. When the other fellow doesn't do it, he's lazy. When I don't do it, I'm busy. When the other fellow does it without being told, he's overstepping his bounds. When I go ahead and do it without being told, that's initiative. When the other fellow states his opinion strongly, he's bullheaded. When I state my opinion strongly, I'm firm. When the other fellow overlooks a few rules of etiquette, he's rude. When I skip a few rules of etiquette, I'm doing my own thing."

But the upshot of making excuses for ourselves — of forgetting our standards just for this time or that time, just for this emergency or that expediency — is that gradually, subtly, we become someone we didn't want to be.

Notice how a teenager named Becky let her standards of honesty slip just once.

The Larsons had a little son with diabetes. His doctor had had some difficulty in stabilizing his insulin injections because of a complicating illness, and the boy had been in and out of the hospital for some weeks. Finally he was allowed home for a few days, and he seemed to be fine. The doctor had one more idea he wanted to try before starting another long series of tests, and he needed a particular drug for it which would have to be flown in from another state.

Because there was a limited supply of this drug and because two other children in the hospital needed it, the doctor released Larsons' son only on the understanding that he could return the day the drug arrived.

Mrs. Larson knew that if the doctor was going to phone her about the arrival of the drug, he would do so before he left his office at 6:00 P.M. She was careful to stay near the phone every day until about that time. Any chance they had to avoid the tediousness and expense of more tests was worth that effort.

On this particular afternoon, Mrs. Larson received a phone call from her husband indicating that his car had broken down and he needed a lift home. Mrs. Larson quickly called Becky and asked her to babysit for her while she ran this errand. She told Becky she might be getting an important call and asked her to be especially careful about messages.

While she was at Larsons', Becky's boyfriend phoned her, and the two chatted for over an hour. When the Larsons returned, Becky told them there had been no phone calls.

"You're certain?" Mrs. Larson asked.

Feeling guilty about the time she'd spent on the phone, Becky replied, "That telephone has done nothing but hang there on the wall."

Six o'clock passed, and Mrs. Larson had no idea that the doctor had tried four times to reach her while the line was busy. She certainly never thought to check in with him since she was assured he could not have phoned. The Larsons' son missed his opportunity to try a new drug and faced another week of expensive tests because Becky defended herself with a lie just once.

When we give ourselves excuses for breaking our standards just this once, or just this year, or just until we're relieved from some pressure, we may find ourselves, as did Becky, in a place we don't want to be. While real life situations are not always as dramatic as the situation in this story, we will lose something dear to us. Slowly, almost imperceptibly, our idealized view of ourselves will slip forever from sight, lost in the fog of bad habits.

Becoming your idealized self, living up to your own standards that are ever before you like the stars, is not impossible. But few people make it because it takes hard, unflinching determination, a determination that views excuses for the feeble friends they are.

Someone said, "The engineer, when he cannot carry his tunnel across or around a mountain, tunnels through it." No excuses. "Impossibilities!" cried Lord Chatham, "I trample upon impossibilities." "Impossible!" exclaimed Mirabeau, "talk not to me of that blockhead of a word. If a man's faith in himself and his mission and his ideals be real and earnest, he cannot fail to gain a certain measure of success. If he does not satisfy the world, he will at least satisfy the voice of conscience. When we look back upon the history of humanity, we see nothing else but a record of what has been achieved by men and women of strong will. No excuses. It is their will that has opened up the way to their fellows. Their enthusiasm of purpose, their fixity of aim, their heroic perseverance — we are all inheritors of what these high qualities have won."

The next time you have an excuse on your lips, or a ready answer for why you can let your ideals slip *this time,* or an explanation why your will is best broken in just this instance, remember that failure rarely happens in one sudden fall. It happens subtly as your best excuses mold you into someone you didn't mean or don't want to be.

HOT AND COLD

One day I was washing my hands and by mistake I turned on just the hot water. Of course, the water was extremely hot, but unfortunately I didn't realize what I had done until my hands were under the water. Well, the dance I did could never be choreographed with any justice. A leap like that has won many an Olympic gold medal.

I have reflected on the incident since then, and I remember something the apostle John said: "I would thou wert cold or hot. So then, because thou art lukewarm, and neither cold nor hot, I will spue thee out of my mouth." (Revelation 3:15-16.)

That's pretty graphic language. It appears that there are some advantages to being hot. I think we can substitute other words in the place of *hot* and understand what the Lord is getting at. Let's change the word *hot* to "actively seeking righteousness and that which is good."

I think you have noticed, with me, that the world is fast being polarized into camps. The good are getting better, and the bad are getting worse. In other words, the hot is beginning to boil and the cold is starting to freeze over. But there are still some — the lukewarm

— who refuse to take a stand. You know the kind. They're the ones who don't stand up for what they believe or who never form an opinion. They can't be bothered to really know the Lord. It's too much work. They love their neighbor — as long as he minds his own business. The lukewarm are those without the courage or heart to really live.

Don Durkee wrote a clever little poem that really puts things in perspective. It's called "Lukewarm."

He was an average kind of guy,
Said the one,
     I agree, said the other.

He was somewhere between a *B*
And a *C* while in school.
     That's not good and not bad,
     Said the other.

His passions were regular
     Didn't stray from the norm?
About average, said the one.
     Not dynamic in sinning,
     Said the other.

Politically he was the middle of the road.
     Didn't cause trouble?
     Asked the other, disappointed.
Didn't cause anything,
Said the one, shaking his head.
     Did he help his neighbor?
About average, not hot and not cold.
     Was he religious?
He wasn't what you'd call unreligious, exactly,
Said the one.
     About average? asked the other.
Right, said the one.
     That's about it then.
     Said the other.

> I don't want him, said heaven.
> Neither do I, said the other.

That verse sums it up, doesn't it? Lukewarm is nothing. It's no life at all. It's living on the fringes of what could be yours. Take out that old thermometer and take your own spiritual temperature. This is one case where the Lord would be happy to have it soar way above normal. Don't assume that no-count attitude that says, "If the Lord is there, I'll meet him sometime," or, "Honesty is a great principle, and I believe in it — when it's convenient."

A friend of mine learned a great lesson from a lovely young lady who lived with his family while completing her studies at a great university. Although she was totally blind, her intellectual and spiritual abilities were unusually keen. She would ask for a telephone number once and she would never forget it. Members of this good family and others who knew this young lady would read textbook assignments to her just once, and yet her test scores were often the highest in the class.

Since my friend was also a student at the university, at the beginning of each semester he would take this young lady and her seeing-eye dog to each new classroom — but only once. That was all she needed. For her, gospel principles needed to be taught and learned only once, and she would live them, all the way, all the time, faithfully.

The lesson she taught my friend had to do with *opened* and *closed* doors. Her pet peeve was someone who would thoughtlessly leave a door only half open — or half closed. Her sense of hearing was so highly developed that a subtle echo from her footsteps would reveal the position of any door she was approaching — except when it stood somewhere in between; and invariably, if it were half open or half closed, she would walk straight into it!

There are those around us who are walking into doors, spiritually speaking, because they refuse to open them all the way. Somehow, our nature sometimes tells us to try to be lukewarm and get away with it — to try to get into heaven by going through the door sideways. Such an attempt is disastrous, because it is impossible.

Bruce Jenner, the Olympic decathlon winner, faced a dilemma as he was deciding whether to train for the decathlon or not. He was having trouble deciding whether to return to college for a second year and train for the decathlon or to work in a professional waterskiing show in Florida, in which case he would never be able to compete again as an amateur. As it happened, he allowed some casual circumstances to make up his mind for him and send him back to college. Thank goodness for whatever those circumstances were, for they have given us a great Olympic runner.

But how many times are we like this undecided college athlete — at a crossroads? Both ways look enticing and we sit and hem and haw, weighing the advantages. We'd like to make no decision — we'd like to go both ways at once. And that's how we feel sometimes about making a commitment to the Lord. Miserably lukewarm. Yet, that misery can be avoided so easily. All we have to do is to take a stand for righteousness; to live the gospel all the way; to make up our minds to be committed 100 percent.

Such an attitude is comparable to the little boy who was asked why he fell out of bed so frequently. His classic reply? "I guess it's because I don't get in far enough." (Adapted from Stan and Sharon Miller, *Especially for Mormons,* vol. 3 [Provo, Utah: Kellirae Arts, 1976], p. 72.) My plea is that you and I will get so involved in the daily living of true principles that we will never fall out. *Never!*

Let me give you a practical challenge that has been given in every age. Joshua said it well: "...Choose you this day whom ye will serve;...But as for me and my house, we will serve the Lord." (Joshua 24:15.)

That's my challenge to you. Let's commit ourselves enthusiastically and consistently to live the gospel of Jesus Christ. Have the courage to get into the fray, the battle of overcoming apathy or fear or laziness. Don't be a coward, standing idly on the sidelines of it all. This is life and it is now, and you were not meant to be bland, tasteless, lukewarm. Choose ye this day! And let that choice be a wholehearted leap to a living of Christ's great commandments, of knowing through prayer the great Father who made you.

MAKING THE MOST
OF TODAY

Two children were playing on a sidewalk when a green caterpillar crawled out from the lawn. "Look at that," said one child, about to smash the creature underfoot. "Wait," said the other child. "Don't smash him; he's going to be a butterfly."

Do you ever feel like a caterpillar — like there is something secret or wonderful or more you could be, but that there are too many obstacles waiting to smash down your best hopes? Each of us feels we would like to emerge from our flawed self and be somebody better or brighter or more worthy of attention. We'd all like to shine in use, achieve some hidden potential, but *all* we see are the *obstacles*. We give ourselves the excuse that we could do *that* or be *this* if things were just different. When this week is over, when this bill is paid, when the kids are grown, when spring comes, we promise ourselves over and over again, things will be different. Just see what we'll do when things change and the obstacles disappear.

But do you know what? Life's obstacles are not likely to disappear. Oh, they may change, or wear new costumes, but life is always full of stumbling blocks. This pressure or frustration may subside, but another pressure or frustration will arise to take its place. If you are waiting for the perfect conditions to become who you want to be, your wait may last forever and your idealized self will be scattered to the wind.

One woman reported that her four-year-old daughter pleaded with her, "Please, Mama, walk with me to the birthday party today." Well, the woman wanted to be a good mother, but she was awfully busy at the moment, and the party was just a block or so away.

"Not this time," the mother said. "I'll just watch you from the porch." So the mother went out and the little girl, dressed in gingham and carrying a birthday present, started down the block. Every few steps she turned around and waved at her mother, to make sure she was still watching. And as the mother watched, the little girl's figure grew smaller and smaller in the distance, still turning every few minutes with a wistful wave.

Then it struck the mother all at once. Just as the little girl had gradually disappeared with distance today, tomorrow she would slowly disappear with time. Her little girl would be gone, irretrievably; the pigtails and childish fancies would be swallowed up with time; the girl would be a woman on a new adventure all her own. Suddenly the mother wanted to take back the last few minutes; she wanted to run the few blocks and clutch the vanishing child. She wanted to make the most of this minute before it had forever fluttered away.

If each of us is going to make the most of today and become who we really want to be, we have to rid ourselves of beliefs that hamper our progress. We have to say good-bye to three fallacies that make us believe tomorrow will be different. (The title of this chapter and the fallacy ideas are taken from "Making the Most of Today," *Relief Society Courses of Study 1978-79* [Salt Lake City: Corporation of the President, The Church of Jesus Christ of Latter-day Saints, 1977], p. 122.)

The first fallacy is the belief that some people don't have any problems or struggles. Do you believe that? It's easy to say *he* and *she* can succeed because *they* don't have my stresses and strains — but is that really true? Do others wear their disappointments and grief on their brow for all to see? No. We all try desperately with one another to put our best foot forward, to give a perfect appearance. The children may be screaming and petulant, but when they go to grandma's they had better put on their best smiles. The bills may be unpaid through second and third notices, but the family well dressed because of charge cards will never admit it. We all put on facades for one another, so no one will know our problems and struggles. Edwin Arlington Robinson's poem about Richard Cory tells of a man who hid some deepset troubles.

Richard Cory

Whenever Richard Cory went down town,
We people on the pavement looked at him:
He was a gentleman from sole to crown,
Clean favored, and imperially slim.

And he was always quietly arrayed,
And he was always human when he talked;
But still he fluttered pulses when he said,
'Good-morning,' and he glittered when he walked.

And he was rich — yes, richer than a king —
And admirably schooled in every grace;
In fine, we thought that he was everything
To make us wish that we were in his place.

So on we worked, and waited for the light,
And went without the meat, and cursed the bread;
And Richard Cory, one calm summer night,
Went home and put a bullet through his head.

(F. O. Matthiessen, ed., *The Oxford Book of American Verse* [New York: Oxford University Press, 1950], pp. 469-70.)

Other people don't have any struggles? Untrue. Don't let yourself be deceived by that dream. Those around you who succeed, who are more loving or more spiritual or more learned than you, have risen *despite* their struggles. You can, too.

The second fallacy that keeps us from making the most of today occurs when we allow circumstances to determine happiness. We believe that if we can just hold on until things improve, happiness will automatically follow. I knew a wife whose husband was in law school. They were miserably poor, always wondering where the next dollar would come from. They lived with their two children on the twentieth floor of a high-rise apartment building, blocks away from grass or swings. Day after day the children, both preschoolers, were cooped up and cranky because there was no place to play except the tiny, dark apartment. The young wife thought, "I'll be so happy when we just have a little grass for the children."

The family finally moved to a bungalow with a yard and the long-awaited grass. The children were wild with joy, but the mother was still not happy.

"Oh, that grass," she said. "It's plagued with spurge and dandelions and fungus. I can't wait until we live someplace that has a decent lawn."

The day finally came. The husband was doing well in his law practice and the family moved to a large new home in the suburbs — this one with a perfect lawn. But the mother was still not happy. Since she could no longer blame the grass, she had to look for another scapegoat — some circumstance that was making her unhappy.

We fool ourselves if we believe that we are happy or unhappy mainly because of the circumstances we find ourselves in. Nothing or no one can make you happy. *You* are the only one who can do that. It is *your* responsibility. Even heaven would not be heaven for you if you hadn't learned this vital art. An ancient prophet tells us this, referring to the judgment bar: "He that is happy shall be happy still; and he that is unhappy shall be unhappy still." (Mormon 9:14.) There it is, plainly written. If you are not fulfilled, look to yourself, not to your circumstances.

And the third false belief that keeps us from making the most of today is this: we erroneously believe that the good life is free of sorrow and pain. That is simply not true. Since our times of best growth often correspond to times of difficulty, why would we want to arrive at that day when all struggle was merely a memory? Haven't you noticed how people, when all is going well for them, will invent a problem, however trivial, just to give their lives meaning? We will never understand beauty or love or happiness if we have no experience with their opposites. There must be opposition in all things.

So let's rid ourselves of these fallacies that stop us from making *today* the day we really live and excel in. Let's stop fooling ourselves that others don't have struggles as we do, that circumstances determine our happiness, that the good life is free of pain. Don't spend an entire life waiting for it all to begin. This is life, here and now. The present moment is the only moment we have to live in. To miss that is to miss it all.

LEARNING TO
LIKE YOURSELF

A man once said to his friend, "I would give half a year's pay to take a two-week vacation from myself." (Adapted from Norman Vincent Peale, *The Tough-Minded Optimist* [Englewood Cliffs, New Jersey: Prentice-Hall, Inc., 1961].) How many of us feel that way? Life is dim and sometimes desperate because we just don't like ourselves. We're painfully aware of all of our faults and shortcomings. We've memorized each flaw. Everywhere we turn we hear, "I just can't do anything right." "Oh, I'm dumb, dumb, dumb." "Nobody likes me." "I'm so ugly."

It's funny, but we may live in the most self-indulgent, yet self-deprecating society in history. Psychologists tell us that the root of most defiant or hostile behavior is simply a lack of self-love. The child who misbehaves, the adolescent who becomes a criminal, the antisocial adult, the woman who can't lose weight, the man who can't cope are usually that way because they do not love or like or respect themselves.

How about you? Do you *like* yourself? Most of us find it somewhat difficult to like ourselves. After all, who has been with you through all of life's embarrassments and follies? Just you. Who was there and watched somewhat critically when you said the wrong thing, arrived at a faulty conclusion, wore something dumb, failed miserably with your best effort? Just you. You've seen yourself get angry when you didn't mean to, break your most earnest resolutions, eat too much. And some of us have been along as we've fallen into real sin. How do you begin to forgive yourself and start again and build a new self-image?

You have to begin by realizing that you can never get away from yourself. You are your constant companion and always have been. You will be with you throughout all eternity. That fact can and will never change. Even those who commit suicide to escape themselves will find they have gained nothing, for you can't escape from yourself. You are stuck with yourself. And that may be your glory or your bane. Since that is the condition of life and all eternity, you have to learn to live with yourself with as much self-respect and self-love as possible. It's a glorious and necessary thing to learn. The results of not doing so will be to dam up your progress from henceforth and forever.

I read in the newspaper some time ago that a woman went out to start her car one morning and found it wouldn't start. Apparently this wasn't an unusual occurrence. In the past her car had died at stop lights in busy intersections and had generally been persnickety. But this morning was too much. She couldn't stand it any more. She couldn't stand being late for one more appointment. She couldn't bear to sit in that car one more minute praying that the motor would turn over. She was fed up. So she got out of her car, found the nearest sledge hammer, and began pummeling her car with all of her pent-up wrath. Over and over she smote the car until it was pocked and scarred with dents. "Ah-ha! Take that!" she must have thought as she acted out her revenge.

I believe that sometimes we get just as frustrated with ourselves as the lady did with her car. We know our faults too well; our bodies or our faces are not as handsome as we'd choose; we've "blown it" a thousand times; so we take it out on ourselves. We purposely frustrate our own efforts. We retreat into laziness or grouchiness or time-wasting.

I think it is significant that Christ's commandment implied a sequence when he instructed us to love our neighbor as ourselves. As hard as we try, we cannot seem to love our neighbor any better than we do ourselves. So our first step in learning to love ourselves is simply this: recognize that you will be with yourself forever, and whether that is a frustrating or fulfilling experience is totally dependent on your mastering the art of self-love. There is no other choice.

The next step in helping you overcome unworthy feelings about yourself is to recognize that you are who you think you are. Nothing is so powerful in shaping your life as your thoughts. As Marcus Aurelius said, "The soul is dyed with the color of its thoughts." The prophets remind us, "As [a man] thinketh in his heart, so is he." (Proverbs 23:7.) What you think upon grows. Therefore, you must study your most likable self and hold it before you as a constant image. If any of us was asked to list his weaknesses and his strengths, we would find that most of us would list far more weaknesses. We revel in weaknesses. We relive painful or disappointing moments in our minds more often than we should.

Longfellow said, "For Time will teach thee soon the truth,/ There are no birds in last year's nest!" Richard L. Evans said it this way: "Often we think of past decisions — of what we should or shouldn't have done. We dwell upon regret and brood about it. Or we think of what we should now be doing and are not doing, of what we would like to learn, and it makes us uneasy.

"We regret misunderstandings — words we wish we hadn't said — words we wish we *had* said — mistakes we have made, people we have offended, opportunities gone by — errors and carelessness that could have been avoided — places we might have gone, things we might have been.

"The past has its place and is valuable for lessons learned. The present also has its place, and what we cannot change should not needlessly keep us from looking and moving forward. Nothing lost or left behind should keep us from now becoming what we can become, from learning what we now can learn." (Richard L. Evans, *An Open Road: Volume III of Thoughts for One Hundred Days* [Salt Lake City: Publisher's Press, 1968], p. 195.)

You are who you think you are. Today is the day to start fresh and like yourself.

The last step to throwing out unworthy feelings about yourself is to consider at length whose child you are. God created you as he did all things on this earth. We read in Genesis that God separated the light from the darkness and called it good; that he made every beast of the field and called each one good. He created you, too, and made the same pronouncement. You are good. Just as every poem or art masterpiece reflects its creator, so do you reflect yours. He would not have you disparage his finest creation.

To the Psalmist who asks this question: "What is man, that thou art mindful of him?" (Psalms 8:4) we ourselves must learn to reply, "I am the Lord's. He created me with care. He endowed me with infinite possibility. I will not be imprisoned by my own self-dislike."

One day a giant of a man, a gypsy, stood by a well, feet apart, drinking deeply. Near him stood a little boy. When the gypsy had finished drinking, he leaned over and looked deep into the well. Curious, the boy tried to pull himself up against the stone rim to see what the gypsy was looking at. The gypsy noticed him, smiled, and scooped the little boy up into his arms.

"Do you know who lives down there?" asked the gypsy. The little boy shook his head. "God lives there," he said. "Look!" and he held the little boy over the edge of the well.

There in the still, mirror-like water, the boy saw his own reflection.

"But that's me!" he told the gypsy.

"Ah," said the gypsy, gently lowering the boy. "Now you know where God lives." (Paraphrased from Stan and Sharon Miller, *Especially for Mormons,* vol. 3 [Provo, Utah: Kellirae Arts, 1976], p. 225.)

May I bear you my testimony that while God may not actually live within us, we are his nearest reflection here on this earth. Our possibilities are staggering. With Shakespeare we must remember: "What a piece of work is man! how noble in reason! how infinite in faculty! in form and moving how express and admirable! in action, how like an angel! in apprehension how like a God!" (William Shakespeare, *Hamlet,* act ii, scene 2.)

The Lord does not want you to dislike yourself. You must begin to throw away unworthy thoughts. You are not a defeated nobody. You have a great and important work to do: the unfolding of your own potential. Let nothing daunt you, for the control of your life is utterly in your hands.

LEARN TO BE CREATIVE

Does it ever seem like some people have all the luck? There's an old song that talks about one lucky fellow. It says, "He should fall down in the mud; he'd come up with a diamond stud." But for most of us it's always the other guy who's lucky — not us.

We often call people lucky, however, when we probably ought to call them creative. All of us are faced with problems and frustrations in life. Those who seem to sail right past their setbacks are those who have learned to use their hidden powers of imagination. Psychologists tell us that we use but a tiny percentage of our brain power. Each of us has a potential beyond our wildest dreams. Consider for a few minutes how you can learn to use your brain more effectively, how you can wake up that spark of genius in you that's just lying dormant.

Here is an example:

One mother of a teenage boy was having a particularly hard time getting him to pick up after himself. His room was always a mess, and he agreed with her that his books and clothing and sports equipment didn't belong strewn all over the living room, but he just never got around to putting things away. She thought about it and decided that one of the reasons it bothered her was that his things got in her way. Since she was picking them up anyway, she began putting them in *his* way. Piles of clothes appeared on the pool table, furry little tennis balls surprised him inside his unmade bed, empty pop cans filled his bathroom drawer, shaving equipment showed up on his desk, school books took up all the space in his gym bag. At first, he just moved things around; after a week or so it became a joke with them. But when, on prom night, he leaned past his date to get his wallet out of the glovebox and found his gym socks there, he knew his time had come. Of his own accord, that boy kept track of his things and the mother never had to bother him again.

Here's another example of creativity put to use. A homeowner whose automatic garage door also turned on a light for him discovered that in the lighted garage he quite often forgot to turn off the car's headlights. He taped aluminum foil on the wall in front of his parking space so the reflection would remind him.

You can learn to be creative like that. You can learn to solve your big problems and your little ones with ease if you'll just utilize your own genius. For most of us, each day is routine — even dull — because we don't invest any of ourselves into it. We eat the same meals, follow the same schedule, even exchange the same chit chat day after boring day. Here are five ways to kindle your creativity, solve old problems, and *live life* more fully.

First of all, be curious. Take a lesson from the child who touches and tastes whatever he seeks — the child who stands on tip-toe, lies on his stomach, or crawls out on a ledge to get a good look at something new. Explore a place you've never been, read a book (or a whole shelf of them) on a topic you know nothing about, get your hands dirty. Learn to discard your preconceptions about any experience and to see the world as brand new each day.

Second — and this follows curiosity closely — ask questions. Never be ashamed to inquire. If you get yourself sunk deep in a problem, try rephrasing the questions you're asking so that they are more open-ended. Learn to live comfortably with questions that seek possibilities rather than to regard each question in life as a demand for *the* right answer. Practice saying "What if . . . ?" and "Why?"

One writer said, "The genius of men like Newton and Einstein lies in that they ask transparent, innocent questions which turned out to have catastrophic answers." For example, the question that young Einstein asked was, "What would the world look like if I rode on a beam of light?" From that question came his entire theory of relativity.

My third suggestion is that you combine ideas. Put things together that don't seem to match; try thinking about one thing in terms of another one.

Robert Frost wrote about the importance of being comfortable with metaphors in order to learn; and I think he was right: comparing the unknown to the known is a tremendous tool in problem-solving. Never lose any of the data you pick up by asking questions: try to keep it all on call — in your head or on paper — so you can use it later on. Don't get too stuck on categorizing ideas — let them mix and influence one another. Be open to new and strange combinations.

Another idea to keep in mind as you try to rekindle your creativity is not to press too hard for too long. Once you've filled your mind with all the information you can gather, once you've explored some new and different combinations of those scraps of information, once you've thought your problem through, back away from it entirely. Play some golf, go for a walk, sleep on it, buy yourself an ice cream cone. Trust that untapped mental resource of yours to work on your problem while you take a break. Many artists and scientists claim that ideas come to them in a flash early in the morning as they wake up, or while they're on vacation, or during some other moment when they're not particularly concentrating.

This isn't to say that you should just wait for inspiration — you *do* have to do some thinking. You may have to go through the process of concentrating and taking a break and then rethinking several times, but that break time will provide your subconscious the chance it needs to help you out.

The fifth way to increase your creativity is to practice being creative. Take some positive action to get out of your mental rut. Surround yourself with creative, challenging people. My dad used to say that if you want to improve, seek out those who will improve you. Join a study group and invest some time in discussion, in the friendly arguing of ideas and alternatives. Change your routine; realign your schedule; set yourself a goal in problem-solving.

Those people who seem lucky are really those who have an interest in life each day and who therefore provide themselves interesting opportunities and choices. You can do that just as well as they can.

The Lord has sent us here to develop our talents and potential, to "Be ye therefore perfect, even as your Father which is in heaven is perfect." (Matthew 5:48.) Let us accept the challenge of becoming perfect by calling forth the creative powers within us.

BEATING THE BLAHS

For many of us January is a downer. The streets seem bleak without Christmas lights; the parties are over; the budget is broken; and winter in all its fury is upon us. It can be a time of the *blahs* — dull, insipid, long, and dark. It's easy to blame your low moods on the month or the weatherman or your job, but why find a scapegoat? This year decide that the blahs won't beat you — you're going to beat the blahs!

Let me give you four ways to liven up your world when it seems a little flat.

First, realize that ups and downs seem to be part of nature's cycle. You have days when life seems to hum merrily along. You have other days when you wish you didn't have to get up. Everybody does. There just seems to be a certain rhythm to existence. I understand from Lesley Conger that a clam has some kind of an inner biological clock so that even if it is transported alive to a laboratory in the prairie, it will still know exactly when the tide is going out on the beach back home. And if the clam stays on the prairie long enough, its internal clock gradually adjusts itself and the clam begins responding to the rhythm of imaginary tides in the prairie. (Lesley

Conger, "Off the Cuff," *The Writer,* September 1978, p. 9.) Amazing? Your body temperature rises and falls on a twenty-four-hour cycle; your stomach contracts roughly every ninety to a hundred minutes. Does it seem so surprising that your emotions run in ups and downs, too? They may not be regular, but they are real.

Don't make the doldrums a habit. Don't embrace depression; send it on its way. You were not meant to be low on energy and enthusiasm.

You still believe in the sun when it slides behind a cloud. When you have the mental blahs, still believe in life's goodness and joy. That belief will put you halfway there.

The second way to beat the blahs is to put your problems in perspective. The traffic jam, the argument, the setback that seems so all-important may not really merit your worry and dismay. Your inner harmony and sense of peace is the most important thing in the world. Don't be so willing to give it up.

I like the story that tells of naturalist William Beebe's visits to Theodore Roosevelt at Sagamore Hill: "Often after an evening's talk the two men would walk over the spreading lawn and look up into the night sky. They would vie with each other to see who could first identify the pale bit of light-mist near the upper left-hand corner of the Great Square of Pegasus, and then either Roosevelt, or Beebe, would recite:

" 'That is the Spiral Galaxy of Andromeda. It is as large as our Milky Way. It is one of a hundred million galaxies. It is two million five hundred thousand light-years away. It consists of one hundred billion suns, many larger than our own sun.'

"Then, after a moment of silence, Theodore Roosevelt would grin and say, 'Now, I think we are small enough. Let's go to bed.' " (Wendell Noble, "The Listener's Digest," KABC, November 20, 1959.)

You are certainly not small, but your problems are. Brush them aside and reconnect with a larger world. Whenever any worry begins to nibble at your contentment, ask yourself, "Is it really worth the price? Can I afford the 'luxury' of a low mood?"

The third way to beat the blahs is to learn something new. Develop a new skill or hobby. Make a new friend. "Curiosity," said editor Frederick Bonfils, "is one of the most permanent and certain characteristics of a vigorous mind. There is no hope for the satisfied man." (Wendell Noble, "The Listener's Digest," KABC, August 1956.)

Has your world become boring because you've been too self-satisfied? Find out that you really aren't a know-it-all. Expose your own ignorance. Learn something new. You live in a world, after all, where the odds against two individuals other than identical twins being exactly alike is a number so high it doesn't even have a name. It would have to be written as 1 followed by 9,031 zeros. You live in a world where butterflies can fly at speeds of twenty miles an hour or more for long distances. Do you know monarchs have been observed within two hundred miles of the coast of England, though they're not native to Europe? You live in a world where dogs are color blind and the average honey bee has to visit over a thousand florets of clover just to fill its honey sac once. If you have the blahs, you need to find out more about this fascinating world in which you live.

The fourth way to beat the blahs involves some reexamination of your life. One day a college girl was lazily walking across campus without any apparent direction when she ran into one of her professors, a man who knew her well. This professor was recognized for his astonishing mind, which seemed to to able to cut through the layers of confusion around a problem and to state it simply. He was a surprisingly small man who would kneel down with his face next to the grass to see the world from a new point of view or who would jump out of grand pianos to greet his music students as they entered class. But this day the professor's interest was on the coed. "What's wrong with you?" he said, eyeing her closely. "You're not yourself."

"Oh, nothing really," answered the girl. "I've just got the blahs."

"I knew it," said the professor, "and I know why. You've worked hard lately, but you have not done one thing all quarter that *really* matters to you, have you? You haven't done one thing that has made you bare your heart. Think about it," he said, and without another word he scurried off.

Let me ask you what the professor asked the girl. Have you done anything lately that really matters to you? You may have been busy, even frantically so, but has any of this activity touched your very soul? Can you say at this point that your life has purpose, that it has a direction that means something to you? Are you really sure why you are here?

Your spirits will go skidding along, never quite taking off, until you feel assured that your existence has meaning. You need to know that all your "busyness" amounts to something. You need to find those moments and those activities that resonate deeply in *your* soul, even if they are not what the world suggests as important.

If you have the blahs, it's time to cut through all of life's fat to its bare bones. Who are you really? Where is the Lord? Talk to him. Break out of old patterns that are dulling your spirit. Take a new inventory of your hours, a sharper classification of what's worth doing and what is just time-killing. When you have filled your life with moments that really matter to you, you'll discover you've beaten the blahs.

REFLECTIONS ON THE
ME GENERATION

An article in *U. S. News and World Report* recorded that today's young adults have found new heroes — themselves. That may be a harsh judgment on today's youth, but more and more observers are calling this the *me* decade, the *me* generation, the *me* society.

Why? Look around and see if you can find examples.

A New York department store opened a "self-center," a telling name for this special section of the shopping area devoted to health foods and cosmetics.

Television transmits the message to us that preoccupation with self — with *my* needs, *my* happiness, *my* gratification — is the highest goal. You've heard the advertisements that say, "You deserve a break today," and, "This I do for me." Other ads feature beautiful women who say they buy the most expensive hair color in the world because "I'm worth it."

Best-selling books sound the same theme, telling people they should be *Looking Out for #1* and *Winning Through Intimidation*.

Old family patterns are disintegrating due to this new trend toward self-indulgence. Social scientists note that many people today are unwilling to make emotional commitments to others. They choose instead to live alone; they choose to live together without the bond — and responsibilities — of marriage; they choose to be childless.

U. S. News and World Report went on to say that "even among couples who choose to have children, there is a change in values. A study by the New York research firm of Yankelovich, Skelly and White, Inc., found that large numbers of parents are self-oriented and are reluctant to make sacrifices for their youngsters."

You know times have changed when the word *fulfillment* is always prefixed with the word *self*.

In a wild, frantic search for self-fulfillment, women are leaving their homes in droves. Many claim that the kind of sacrifice necessary to rear a family is boring and meaningless. As one writer said, spending one's time bringing up children is ridiculous because "children come up the same, brought or not." Slogans of the day include "End human sacrifice, don't get married" — and, courtesy of the proabortionists, "Keep your laws off my body."

As this kind of evidence piles up, I fear we are moving ever so subtly into a world where we are taught to see others strictly in terms of what they can do for us; where we are conditioned to put indulgence before conscience; where we grope blindly for meaning, having abandoned any meaning that originates outside of our own needs.

It's in a value-free world, a world with no absolute ideals, that all decisions swing around the two poles called "me" and "now."

One woman who tried group therapy as a means to self-understanding said, "As a member of the 'me' society, I am committed to looking after my own emotional ego needs."

Well, who can knock the goal of enhanced self-understanding, of self-fulfillment, of self-love? Even the scriptures tell us to love our neighbors as *ourselves,* implying that we have to love ourselves before we can do much good for anyone else. What's wrong, then, with this new preoccupation with self? Simply this: it doesn't work. *Selfishness* was never *happiness*. Try desperately to please yourself, to make yourself happy, to fulfill your every whim, and the result will always be misery. Happiness may seem to come just within your reach when you focus on getting it for yourself, but, like a too-early moth, it will always fade away.

Another scripture sheds light on this mysterious law of life. The

Lord tells us that "... he that loseth his life for my sake shall find it." (Matthew 10:39.) The journey to self-love, self-esteem, and self-respect was never made in a ship called self-preoccupation.

To truly find your life, you must give it to something greater than yourself. You must find the Lord, a God that is greater than your own image; you must remember others, a thought more enlarging than the shrinking concerns of one ego.

For each of us there must come the moment when all our mirrors turn into windows. That is the moment of growing up. The adolescent looks inward; the adult can look outward.

Do you want to love yourself? We all do. For her less serious works, Edna St. Vincent Millay used the *nom de plume* Nancy Boyd. A volume of the Nancy Boyd pieces was published with a preface by Edna, who wrote that she was Nancy Boyd's earliest admirer. "I take pleasure in recommending to the public these excellent small satires," she said, "from the pen of one in whose work I have a never-failing interest and delight." To find this never-failing interest and delight in your own life, even in your own self, give yourself to something great. Give yourself to the Lord and to his plan of happiness for you. Give yourself to others.

One man in his twenties who overcame a background of street violence and drugs to go to college and run a youth program at his neighborhood church explained: "Unless you are committed to a marriage or to a way of life, you become bored, tired, and disgusted. Unless there is a commitment, it is easier to walk away from things than to see them through."

Throughout the history of civilization, mankind has had one paramount weakness. It hasn't been murder, dishonesty, or even adultery. It has been idolatry. Even while Moses was up on the mountain receiving the Ten Commandments, the children of Israel were below him busily fashioning a golden calf. Modern man suffers from that same softness — idolatry. We're much too sophisticated to craft golden calves, but we have idols all the same. Those idols are ourselves. If we made images of ourselves and danced and pranced before them and sacrificed all good things to them, we would be no less foolish than we already are.

It is this idol — this belief that "I am the measure of all things" — that has made America's students flounder and fall as they take national tests, as millions of them graduate from high school with inadequate reading skills. Why be concerned with merit if life has no meaning besides what I give it?

It is this idol — this belief that "I am the measure of all things" — that has turned whole pockets of our cities into porno-playgrounds and see-it-all movies. Why not indulge if it arouses my senses?

It is this idol — this belief that "I am the measure of all things" — that is responsible for a declining work ethic, increased absenteeism, and substandard performances on the part of workers. Why work so hard, if it gives me no pleasure *now*?

Now is the time for all of us to tear down the false idol of self that can so easily dominate our landscapes. As a wise man once said, "Men who deserve monuments do not need them."

If you would truly love yourself, change all your mirrors to windows and lose your life for others, for ideals, and for the Lord, that you may find your life once again.

PART TWO

THE MEASURE
OF HOME

A CHAMPION FAMILY

One spring in Cypress Gardens, Florida, there was a special display of championship that will not soon be forgotten. It was the barefoot waterskiing contest. There, ready for the opening event, was Billy, looking much like any other fourteen-year-old boy, except that his shoulders were much more developed from hours of workouts. He stood calmly on the dock as a speedboat circled the inlet. As the boat neared, he stepped confidently onto a water ski waiting there, one foot balancing easily behind the other. The boat roared off and he rode the turbulence with steady confidence. Three-quarters of the way around the designated circle, he pulled his left leg from the water ski and lightly dropped it, ready for the painful, nearly impossible rigors of barefoot waterskiing; the tender soles of his feet ripped against the water as he sped along.

That afternoon, many barefoot skiers had gone only a few rods before they tumbled, but Billy's heels were cutting the water evenly and firmly. He held the tow rope while his body leaned at a forty-five-degree angle back from the bar.

His short blonde hair was drenched and the flying spray from his body at times obscured sight of him. Average barefoot waterskiing times before his had been one and a half to three minutes; after that duration some slight shift in body weight or some extra water roughness tumbled the barefoot skiers end over end into the lagoon. But Billy kept hanging grimly in there. The announcer kept the crowd posted on the time: four minutes; four and three-quarters minutes; five minutes; and finally five and a half minutes — an outstanding time, better than almost all the men had been able to do.

The best two runs of the day determined the water skier's score. Billy's second run was the last one for the day. The sun was low in the sky as he started his final test. Knowledgeable people say the friction of the water at the high speed necessary to ski barefoot can cut the flesh right off the heel. Billy had trained for this, though, and his feet were toughened by hours of barefoot skiing. One T-shirt in the crowd sagely proclaimed, "Barefoot skiers have more sole." Probably so, but that, too, takes preparation.

Billy began his circle around the lagoon with perfect style. His body straightened at a right angle against the ski tow bar. About once during each circle he held with one hand while he laced his fingers through the spray — first one hand, then the other. "Watch it Billy, you're doing great; don't let anything make you lose that delicate balance!" came a voice from the crowd.

Again the four-minute time was passed. Could he repeat his outstanding morning performance? Five minutes, five and a half, six minutes, seven minutes. The grandstand crowd was on its feet, cheering: "Hang in there Billy! You can make it!"

Eight minutes. Billy's body flashed past the stands. Eight and three-quarters minutes! The three-year-old endurance record was broken. "Billy boy! Go, Billee, go!" Could this young man hang on one more lap? Incredibly he did. Another lap. Then another. The crowd's excitement filled the lagoon. As Billy went by he raised a triumphant arm to someone in the grandstand. Nine minutes; ten; eleven. Unbelievable.

"Go, Billy! Hang in there!" Billy's slight frame was carrying the spirit of mankind. Where did he get the will to go on when others around him had failed?

"Go, Billy; go for all of us." Finally, after twelve minutes and four grueling seconds, he tumbled into the dark water.

The crowd watched as Billy was brought to shore. How would his feet be? He stepped ashore and was surrounded by well-wishers and the press. Here was a champion. But the story does not end here.

Later, as we were leaving the area, we learned who Billy had motioned to in the grandstand as he lifted his arm in triumph. We watched as his family — those who had urged and supported and inspired him — surrounded him. A mother, a father, two sets of grandparents, and two younger children all piled into a visibly aging car, the children sitting on the laps of those nearest the doors. It took three slams to manage to latch the door with so many people inside. The car sputtered a couple of times and, sagging, eventually rolled away. That family knew Billy was a winner and they were all there to support him. They had always been there, believing in him as long as he could remember, coming to cheer for him no matter what the heat or discomfort, in a crowded, worn-out car.

Their laughter and love floated back from the car as they drove away. Yes, there was a display of championship that day: a champion family.

All of us struggle to be champions in one way or another. We live in a star-conscious world. Weekly magazines that tell us about the lives of the famous are bestsellers. We hold our breath for the Olympian who earns a perfect score, for the runner who breaks the world record for the hundred-yard dash, for the football heroes who run the touchdowns at the Super Bowl.

But in all our worshiping of the world's champions — in all our struggles to be champions ourselves at work, at a sport, in a field of knowledge — let us not forget that most important contest of all. Against all the forces of a society that would pull against it, let us be the ones to create champion families. Though you may not be written up in a magazine for it, though you may not be given shiny trophies to put on a shelf for your efforts, the rewards will be infinite. It was Sir John Bowring who said, "A happier family is but an earlier heaven." (Stan and Sharon Miller, *Especially for Mormons*, vol. 2 [Provo, Utah: Kellirae Arts, 1973], p. 117.) And the converse is true, too. How often have we seen a person at the top of his career, with all the power and glory that money can bring, cry out that he is miserable because he doesn't have a happy family?

There is no more important work you will ever do than what you do at home. We all know, after all, that the best source of good people is still a good family. The government may take your tax dollar to create institutions to take the family's place; our society may try in vain to create agencies to reform those who are delinquent. But how much better it is to shape a human being from birth in a loving family, than to try to reshape him when his life has fallen apart because his family did not care.

I was amused once to hear a group of men discussing the names — the handles — they use on their citizen-band radios. One said he was the Skywalker; another called himself Double Dart; but the handle I'll always remember is the one mentioned last: "I'm the Family Man."

Are you a family man, a family woman? Does your family really come first with you?

Children grow up; they grow away from us; they become independent adults. This is as it should be. But if you want those adults you raise to reflect and carry on all the highest values you can give them, the time to start is when they are young, while they are at home and within hugging distance.

Billy's family didn't just show up to see him win: they were with him when he was learning, when he was practicing.

Champion families are built day by day, through little gestures of love and support. Try to see today's action, today's decision, in view of its most far-reaching implication. Put your energies now into attaining those most important long-range goals. Seek first a champion family. Other awards just tarnish.

FOUR GIFTS YOU OWE YOUR CHILDREN

A twenty-four-year-old Colorado man once sued his parents for $350,000, charging that their failure made him what he was. While this sounds extreme to us, there aren't many parents who haven't worried whether they are doing right by their children. Parents blame or praise themselves for their child's disposition, school performance, health, talents, or sense of responsibility. They buy books to learn how to feed and rear their child, or they consult weekly columns on how to get along with their child. Sometimes the burden can be overwhelming because we want so desperately to do a good job.

But ironically, though we want to do a good job, we still approach the whole task of child-rearing pretty haphazardly. Can you imagine trying to build a house without a blueprint, a set of plans to determine your directions? Can you imagine teaching a class without any idea of what you wanted to say? Would you write a thesis without an outline? Those people and institutions that really excel in this world are the ones that work according to specific goals. We should use this success tool in teaching and rearing our children.

Have you ever stopped and really asked yourself what particular qualities you wanted to instill in your child? I know a young couple who sat down and made a list of skills and qualities they wanted their child to acquire. The list was basic, including such things as honesty and kindness. But they also included particular opportunities they hoped they could give their child, such as music lessons or outdoor experiences. While such a list may sound elementary, this couple reported that with their goals specifically defined they could plan activities for their child and they could reinforce ideals with new direction and commitment. They knew where they were going and they could measure their progress.

The story is told of a woman who entered her flower garden in a local green-thumb contest. When two judges arrived one afternoon, she quickly took them to the rear of her home, where she proudly led them through her garden. Sensing somehow that the judges were dissatisfied with her entry, she asked how well others had done with their projects.

"Madam," replied the more officious of the two judges, "your garden doesn't compare at all favorably with other entries. Your garden is sparsely planted — and the various plants, though well selected, are not nearly as mature as others we have seen."

"Yes," cried the woman in exasperation, "others may have prettier flowers, but you'll not find a better tended garden." The judge, failing to understand what the woman was saying, asked for clarification.

"I planted my garden late in the season," she explained. "This patch of ground had become totally overgrown with weeds. I worked for days to clear the ground. Before I was half finished, the remaining weeds began to shed their seeds, and soon new weeds started to grow where I had scarcely cleared the ground. Even after I had planted my flowers the problem of weeds continued to beset me. I have been so busy keeping the patch clear of weeds that I have not had much time to water and cultivate my flowers."

"My good woman," replied the judge, "you have forgotten one essential thing: we never award blue ribbons for weeding. We're looking for beautiful flowers. In fact, you would do well to discover one important principle: where the ground is covered with lush, well-tended flowers, weeds don't seem to thrive nearly as well. I would advise you to become more concerned with flowers than with weeds." (*D&C Self-Instruction Program*, vol. 2 [Salt Lake City: The Church of Jesus Christ of Latter-day Saints], p. 17.)

The same holds true for parents. Plant flowers — don't just pluck weeds. Those who are busy helping their offspring cultivate positive characteristics and skills do not often have idle, misbehaving children. After all, the child whose mother is helping her bake cookies is not going to be drawing on the wall at that time in a bid for attention.

So when all is said and done, what gifts of character do you want your children to inherit from your presence with them? What flowers are you planting in their souls? May I suggest just four gifts you owe your children?

First, you owe your children a sense of responsibility. Growing up means that your children will not always have you to do things for them. You will not always be there to make their decisions and to soften the blows, and you wouldn't want to be. Each child must know that his actions have consequences; that these consequences sometimes profoundly affect his own life and the lives of others. One mother I know helped her daughter learn this by allowing her child to feel the natural consequences of her own acts. If her daughter, who was clearly old enough to dress herself, was not ready when the bus came for school, the bus left without her, leaving her to walk and arrive late. How many times do you think that happened?

Part of teaching children responsibility for themselves may involve cooperative planning for them to do certain chores around the house, and then holding them to it. The adult world would soon fall apart if people didn't take their assignments seriously. Train your children early to be responsible for their jobs.

Second, you owe your children inner security and self-confidence. Analyze very carefully how you speak to them. They will only become as radiant as you believe them to be. Do you find yourself saying to your children, "You *always* spill your milk," or, "Can't you remember *anything*?" Do you ever imply that they are stupid or insignificant or just plain bothersome? It's easy to slip into the habit of merely ordering your children around instead of talking to them. You owe your children the self-confidence that comes from knowing someone wholeheartedly believes they are wonderful.

Third, you owe your children standards and rules to live by — standards that give their lives meaning and purpose and boundaries. Children really need and want rules. They are happier for them. And don't just limit these to family rules. Teach your children that they have a Father in heaven who loves them. Teach them that he loves them so much he has given them some heavenly rules or commandments that, when followed, bring joy and security.

"There is a story about four clergymen who were discussing the merits of the various translations of the Bible. One liked the King James Version best because of its simple, beautiful English.

"Another liked the American Revised Version best because it is more literal and comes nearer to the original Hebrew and Greek.

"Still another liked Moffat's translation because of its up-to-date vocabulary.

"The fourth minister was silent. When asked to express his opinion, he replied, 'I like my mother's translation best.'

"The other three expressed surprise. They did not know that his mother had translated the Bible. 'Yes, she did,' he replied. 'She translated it into life, and it was the most convincing translation I ever saw.' " (From *Saints' Herald,* quoted in Stan and Sharon Miller, *Especially for Mormons,* vol. 1 [Provo, Utah: Kellirae Arts, 1971], p. 268.)

Like this mother, give your children the gift of standards and rules and the knowledge that they have a Father in heaven who loves them.

The *fourth* gift you owe your children is the courage to win. Life is full of knocks for all of us. Though you'd like to, you cannot guarantee your children that they will have only sunshine days. Give them instead the courage to never give up. Remember that success consists not in never falling, but in rising every time you fall.

You do not wholly shape your children. Everyone who has ever been a parent knows that babies have distinct personalities all their own. But you can plant flowers in their souls. You can very consciously help them develop traits that will bless their lives for years to come. Don't let *your* children be the ones who look at themselves and want to sue you for damages.

HOUSE AND HOME
PAYMENTS

One day I was involved in the
monthly ritual that so many of us follow: making the house payment.
In these days of inflation, that can be a painful moment. We think,
"Oh, there goes half my salary." But if we want a house to live in, one
that we can call our own, we've got to pay the price. Well, as I was
writing that check for the house payment, a question struck me with
such force that I stopped writing and stared into space. It was short —
only six words — but it was potent. *"Have you made your home
payment?"*

Let me explain. If you make regular house payments over a
period of time, you'll someday own your house. It may take years,
but someday it will be yours. Well, just as we must make regular
payments in dollars to secure a house, so we must make regular
investments in love, patience, consideration, and kindness to make
our house a home. We must pay for a house. We must pay for a
home. All worthwhile things demand their price. Have *you* made
your regular home payment?

Let me tell you about a young man who learned to invest in his
home.

Dave had just begun his career as an architect. His hours were long, and frequently he brought work home to finish. On this particular evening he had been at the desk steadily, except for a quick dinner, since he arrived home. He glanced up to see the eyes of his two-year-old son, Matthew, peering at him across his papers. He knew the eyes were accompanied by sticky little fingers.

"Go ask Mommy to wash your hands, Matt," he told him, and immediately turned back to his work.

In no time, it seemed, Matt was back, fingering the ink bottle (which Dave moved abruptly) and working his way around to lean against his dad's chair. Matt began to rock gently.

"Back off, Matt," Dave said irritably. "Leave Daddy alone."

"Story?" Matthew asked hopefully, reaching for the corner of Dave's blueprint.

"No, Matthew. Now get lost!"

Matt disappeared, and for a few minutes Dave worked in peace. Finally he glanced up to see his little son huddled on the floor in the doorway, his blanket bunched around him and tears in his eyes. Matt's left thumb was in his mouth, and with his right hand he gently rubbed his cheek with the corner of the ragged blanket. He looked so desolate, so hurt and vulnerable, that for a moment Dave felt the tears begin to rise in his own eyes.

It was then, in that moment, that Dave saw suddenly and clearly and with a deep sense of humility what a very powerful figure he was in little Matt's life. Matthew didn't need a story; he wasn't overwhelmed with curiosity about ink bottles; he was not bent on destroying the careful placement of lines on blueprints: Matthew simply wanted to be near his father. Nobody else would do for Matt just then, and the little comfort he derived from his blanket was not enough. There were countless architects who could respond to the mute demands of a design problem, but there was only one person in the world who could answer Matt's need for his daddy's attention.

In a flash, Dave envisioned a Matthew grown beyond the solace of a few minutes with his dad, a Matthew whose immediate need might not be filled by so simple a thing as a story. He understood that if he were to be able to help his grown son at all, that relationship would have to be built with his baby son. The time for Matt was *now;* blueprints don't grow up.

"Hey, tiger," Dave said quietly, removing the tip from his pen, "how about walking out to the garden with me? Maybe we could find ourselves a strawberry or two."

Matt's eyes lit up, even though tears still glistened on his cheeks. Leaving his blanket in a heap, he rode his daddy's shoulder out into the summer evening.

That's what I call a home payment.

I have a good friend who was reared by a mother who made home payments every night. She would take her small son on her lap just before bedtime and read to him out of the very best books: children's stories from the Bible and great children's literature like *Heidi* and *Gulliver's Travels*. As Strickland Gillian once put it:

> Richer than I you can never be —
> I had a mother who read to me.

(Richard L. Evans, *Richard Evans' Quote Book* [Salt Lake City: Publishers Press, 1971], p. 13.)

Another home payment is made.

When we make regular home payments with our wives and husbands, our sons and daughters, we send a message more powerful than words. I am reminded of an analogy I once heard. A father was plowing his field near a canal bank while his son played there.

Suddenly the child shouted, "Help! I've fallen in the canal!"

The father looked up from his plowing to see his son hanging on to a small willow that grew on the slippery bank.

"Hang on, son," the father reassured. "Hang on until I plow another round!" (Bert M. Williams.)

Ridiculous? What father would leave his son struggling against a swift-running stream of water, fighting for his very life? And yet many fathers place their work ahead of their son's welfare — never quite voicing the words, but saying by their attitude, "Hang on, son, while I plow another round."

Regular home payments will save many a child. If we could somehow just remember the spirit of this verse:

> A careful man I ought to be —
> A little fellow follows me.
> I do not dare to go astray,

For fear he'll go the selfsame way.
I cannot once escape his eyes.
Whate'er he sees me do, he tries.
Like me he says he's going to be,
The little chap who follows me.
He thinks that I am good and fine,
Believes in every word of mine.
The base in me he must not see,
The little chap who follows me.
I must remember as I go,
Through summer's sun and winter's snow,
I'm building for the years to be
The little chap who follows me.

                                          (*Millennial Star.*)

The Lord has given us some advice about home payments. It's not only advice, it's a promise:

"There is a law, irrevocably decreed in heaven before the foundations of this world, upon which all blessings are predicated —

"And when we obtain any blessing from God, it is by obedience to that law upon which it is predicated." (D&C 130:20-21.)

What that boils down to is this: when we make the payment we get the blessing. That's a pretty sobering thought. If we want a real home, we will have to make up our minds to pay the price. And the price is worth it.

Houses *can* become homes. I have seen it happen, even in families who really didn't start trying until the kids were teenagers (or even later). But the Lord is serious about families and his promise is sure. If we'll make *regular* home payments with our families, changes will occur. They may be slow, but they *will* come. That's the way the Lord wants it. House payments without home payments are useless — but home payments, even on the humblest rented apartment, will bring eternal dividends.

I'D RATHER BE
A FATHER

Do you know how to make a real mark in the world, how to have some kind of an influence that will outlast your short stay here? This quest has been a drive that has motivated men for centuries. Men have built monuments to themselves, have commissioned artists to paint their pictures, have strived to be remembered here for some unusual trait — all so that they can be assured that their life has not been lived in vain. Buried within most personalities is this aim given words by William James: "The greatest use of life is to spend it for something that will outlast it."

I thought of those words when I heard the funeral oration of a prominent man in our community. Written by his daughter, it went like this:

"The paper says our father died, but we know that he lives. We see him still in this daughter's compassion and that grandson's name, in this son's extra inch that makes him stand above the crowd and in that granddaughter's deep brown eyes. Our father lives, and we'll see him each time a son squares his shoulders to accept responsibility, each time his children laugh at their discouragements and refuse to give up. Daddy's love for us is like the charge that holds the particles of an atom together. They may not touch, but the binding power between them is the strongest in the universe. Our father lives, and his lessons have changed our eternities."

As I looked at his beautiful children and grandchildren standing like a bastion of mutual support for one another during their time of sorrow, I thought, "Here is a man who has made a mark on the world. Here is a man who was first a father."

In our world of fast-paced careers, executive ladders that beg to be climbed, and desks that never quite get cleared of their work, we forget this most important responsibility — our children. And yet when all is said and done, what else matters? Everything else fades with time except those extraordinary human beings you've had a hand in creating.

Eliot Daley wrote this about being a father: "Women may be tired of being regarded, culturally, as housekeepers and diaper washers; well, I'm tired of being culturally regarded as a breadwinner. . . .

"I do extraordinarily interesting things in my work. I really love it. And I earn plenty enough to get by. [But] I care more about how my children emerge than I do about how big my business gets. . . .

"I'd rather be a father." (Eliot A. Daley, *Father Feelings* [New York: William Morrow and Company, Inc., 1978], pp. 110-11.)

One of our country's most noted generals — a man who commanded hundreds of thousands with an order, who literally held the fate of a nation in his hands — put fatherhood as a top priority. General Douglas MacArthur kept behind his desk a plaque titled, "A Father's Prayer."

"Build me a son, O Lord, who will be strong enough to know when he is weak; and brave enough to face himself when he is afraid, One who will be proud and unbending in defeat, but humble and gentle in victory.

"Build me a son whose wishes will not replace his actions, a son who will know Thee, and that to know himself is the foundation stone to knowledge. Send him, I pray, not in the path of ease and comfort, but stress and spur of difficulties and challenge; here let him learn to stand in the storm, here let him learn compassion for those who fall.

"Build me a son whose heart will be clear, whose goal will be high; a son who will master himself before he seeks to master others:

One who will learn to laugh, yet never forget how to weep; one who will reach into the future, yet never forget the past, and after all these things are his; this I pray, enough sense of humor that he may be serious, yet never take himself too seriously. Give him humility so that he may always remember the simplicity of true greatness, the open mind of true wisdom, the meekness of true strength; then I, his father will dare to whisper, 'I have not lived in Vain.' '' (Stan and Sharon Miller, *Especially for Mormons,* vol. 1 [Provo, Utah: Kellirae Arts, 1971], p. 25.)

"Build me a son, a daughter, like that, O Lord" — these thoughts should certainly command our prayerful hours. But I seem to hear the Lord answering that kind of prayer with this: "I have given *you my* child for a season to guide him through his mortal experience. With my help, *you* build me a son who will be strong enough to know when he is weak and brave enough to face himself when he is afraid. *You* build *me* a son; *you* build *me* a daughter."

For fathers, you who struggle against such pressures to provide for your family, it is not enough to prescribe the child you want and close your eyes and hope he will appear. It will never happen. The coin of character stamped upon your child will be the one you put there.

What does this mean in a practical sense? It means an investment of your time, your thought, and your sacrifice. It may mean a reexamination of your priorities. One wit made a comment that has become too true for America's children. "Paternity," he said, "is a career that is imposed upon you one fine morning without any inquiry as to your fitness for it. That is why there are many fathers who have children, but very few children who have fathers."

The father whose daughter so beautifully eulogized him repeated a comment often in his forty-five years of fathering: "When your child needs help is when he needs it, not some other time." That father missed work or gave up personal activities to watch his children perform; drove sons at 5:00 A.M. on stormy mornings to deliver newspapers; sat his daughters on his lap until his legs ached, reading and rereading their favorite bedtime stories; listened when his children wanted to talk; noticed when a married daughter living far away couldn't afford a Thanksgiving turkey and sent money for the feast, watched and cared and cared and watched through a lifetime for his children. Convenient? Never, for he was a man whose career was just as demanding as yours. Thousands looked to him for leadership. But if we wait until it's convenient or until it fits into our schedule to be fathers, fathers we will never be.

Make your mark on the world — in the hearts of your children. All the thousands of shallow indentations you make elsewhere may fade, but your children will carry you with them always.

THE GIFT THAT
KEEPS ON GIVING

Do you remember the old lyric that says, "The song is over, but the melody lingers on..."? I've often thought of how many things in life are like that — we feel their influence long after their presence is taken from us. The sun, for example, is one of those kinds of things. It shines all day on us and then disappears beyond the horizon to leave us in darkness for hours. But while it shines it warms the earth so much that we can tolerate its absence without freezing to death. We feel the sun's warmth even when the skies are black.

Stars are in the same category. Scientists tell us that some of the stars we view in our nighttime skies may have exploded into space thousands — even millions — of years ago, and that those stars are long extinct. We can see them because the light they sent out all those years ago is just barely reaching our planet. There is no star, but the light keeps shining on.

And mothers — they're in the same category. Long after we may have grown beyond needing their actual physical care, their reminders to wear our boots or eat our vegetables — their influence — keeps shining in our lives. Whether we live thousands of miles away or our last touch with them was decades ago, the song may be over, but the melody lingers on.

As the children in Temple Bailey's fable say of their mother, "We cannot see her, but she is with us still. A mother like ours is more than a memory. She is a Living Presence." (Richard L. Evans, *Richard Evans' Quote Book* [Salt Lake City: Publishers Press, 1971], p. 13.)

Why is a mother's love so profound, so irreplaceable? I think it's because in a hurried, careless world where so many have so little time for us, there is one who has always believed we were worth her hours of effort. There is one who loved us irrationally, even when we didn't deserve to be loved. There is one who has always believed we were far better than we really are. That one is Mother. And against all the awkward knocks of an awkward world, her love has been a shield, a guide, and a gift. It's a gift that keeps on giving.

C. S. Lewis, in his superb autobiography *Surprised by Joy*, mentions his mother but briefly. He tells us that she started him in both French and Latin when he was only a child. And then, while he was still very little, she died. But his comment about her death is revealing. He says: "With my mother's death all settled happiness, all that was tranquil and reliable, disappeared from my life. There was to be much fun, many pleasures, many stabs of Joy; but no more of the old security. It was sea and islands now; the great continent had sunk like Atlantis." (C. S. Lewis, *Surprised by Joy: The Shape of My Early Life* [New York: Harcourt, Brace and Company, 1955], p. 21.)

Certainly mothers supply us the gift of security. One writer described a mother's gifts this way: "A mother is a person who sees that there are only four pieces of pie for five persons and promptly remarks that she's never cared for pie."

But the gifts I remember best from my mother are the ones that were uniquely hers to give because, like all mothers, she is a person unlike any other in the world. My mother is humorous and tiny and believes she's capable of nearly anything, even though she's past eighty. I love her spirit. I dropped in to visit her one day and she was back in her yard planting her spring garden. The ground was hard and crusted over with months of lying fallow, but she was out there — all five feet two inches and ninety pounds of her — swinging a pick to cut through the crust.

Her humor has given *me* the saving grace to laugh my way out of crises whenever they flare in my life. I remember her saying that when I was a child we had many round-table discussions in our home: "I had to chase Paul round and round the table."

She is an accomplished artist. I have a picture — a mountain scene — hanging in my office, that she painted when she was in her seventies. And every time I look at it, I remember not only how much she loves life, but how she's made me love it, and laugh with it, and never give up. Now that's a gift that keeps on giving, and always will, even though I rarely see her due to distance.

One young woman told me of a gift *her* mother gave that kept on giving and giving. It seems when my friend was young her mother poured a rich imagination into creating a series of stories about a squirrel named Bosky who lived near their house. The mother told this girl stories every day at lunchtime before she went to school, and the stories were always wildly suited to the day and the child and the child's present need.

All that was in her distant past when the girl — now grown into a young woman — began substitute teaching in the inner-city schools. Each day the routine for her was the same. She would call the district to say she was available to substitute teach, and in a few minutes they would call back with her assignment for the day. Each morning she was assigned to a different school; each morning she was a stranger in the classroom.

One particular morning was destined to be rough. As she walked into the classroom, she could see that the kids were out to get the substitute. They were tough kids — some of them violent — and she was left all alone with them for the day without any lesson plan or any idea about what they were supposed to study.

She tried everything during that long day of substitute teaching to get their attention, but they called her names and threw spitwads at her, and some of them wandered right out of the classroom. "Please don't throw your papers on the floor," she said, as the floor became knee-deep in litter. "I'll call the principal," she said. And they laughed, "Who cares?" Fights broke out between students, and she seemed helpless to stop them. Finally it happened: the point of no return. A fire started in an apartment building a block away and one of the students in the room caught sight of it out of the window.

"Wow, look," he said. "Let's go." The little substitute teacher was horrified as every one of the students began running out of the classroom to watch the fire. She wanted to throw her body across the door to stop them. Anything. But she was powerless. It was quite clear that she had failed. There was no doubt about it — she had totally lost control and would probably never be hired to teach again.

In total dismay, she walked out of the building to find the kids, and as she did she caught sight of a squirrel. In a situation like that a squirrel would have been no help to you or me, but to her it meant something special. Her mind suddenly traveled back in time and space to the little girl she had been, listening to stories about a squirrel named Bosky. And she remembered other things, too. She remembered that her mother had said, "I don't wish you easy days and easy victories, for that isn't likely to happen in life. But I do wish that every time you fall down you can get up again. I wish you courage." And she remembered that when her mother had been stricken with palsy and the left side of her face had been paralyzed for a year her mother had never succumbed to self-pity, but had instead been courageous and positive and full of faith. So the young woman gathered her courage from some unknown corner of her heart, picked up her head, and continued to teach, becoming a master teacher who influenced hundreds with her skill. Courage and faith in herself — that was a gift from her mother, a gift that very obviously kept on giving.

The song is over, but the melody lingers on. We all love and need our mothers forever. And it's not because we can't take care of ourselves — we all grow big enough — but because we draw from their love and their spirit something that fills us with the strength to walk on when they are no longer there to carry us.

The Lord said it simply: "Honour thy father and thy mother." (Deuteronomy 5:16.)

PREPARING FOR ETERNITY

When I was a soldier coming home from World War II, I saw a beautiful sight as our boat docked. There were moms and dads and sweethearts and brothers and sisters, all waiting for a glimpse and a hug of their own soldier boy who had been gone so long. For some the separation had been only months, but for most of us it had been years. The entire crowd seemed to swell with anticipation as the boat anchored. Here and there were cheerful, homemade signs that proclaimed for special eyes to see, "Welcome Home, Bob" (or John or Jack).

I liked to watch families greet their long-away members. The mother was usually first — there was no containing her behind the barriers, her arms so anxious to hold her boy once again. She'd invariably break loose at first sight of the face she had missed so long. Brothers and sisters would follow. The older ones were proud, shy, even a little timid; the younger ones would clamor for his attention. And there, last in line, quietly waiting for his turn, would be Dad, a father standing a little taller than he had been just minutes earlier. He'd patiently skirt the edge of the group, finally getting to shake the soldier's hand with an expression that said more eloquently than words ever could: "I'm proud you're mine."

Since that time I've seen similar scenes reenacted all over the world as sons or daughters or loved ones return home from school or other adventures that have taken them far away. You've seen it, too: tearful good-byes, joyous welcomes, parents clinging to children, wives in the arms of husbands, teenagers nervously laughing, hands gripping hands, emotions spilling over, people caring. Somehow airports and train stations bring out our deepest feelings, and things we haven't had courage to say finally get said and feelings we've been afraid to show finally get expressed. All of a sudden, as the prospect of losing that loved one — even temporarily — becomes real, we realize how terribly we care.

Have you ever wondered why we're like that? We can go along complacently, and suddenly — for some reason — we're shocked into the realization that our dad or mom, brother or sister, son or daughter is really more important than we ever wanted to admit. Death often prompts that awakening. We see someone slipping from us and we want to clutch them back, hold them to us, knowing that life will never be the same again without them.

Life here is just a shadow of what eternity is like. The reason people in families feel so deeply — consciously or unconsciously — about each other is simply this: our Father in heaven intends that families should last forever. I repeat: families should last forever. Just imagine the warmth and security and happiness that can abound when husbands and wives and children belong to each other forever. It reminds me of a favorite song, "I'll Be Loving You." The younger generation may not remember it, but it has great lines. One phrase goes something like this: "I'll be loving you always, with a love that's true . . . always. Not for just an hour; not for just a day; not for just a year; but always." That's the way the Lord intends it to be.

I think you can catch the spirit of eternal caring in the final minutes of the Savior's life. There he was, the greatest of all, our elder brother, in pain so intense we cannot comprehend it. And yet, can you remember what he said when he saw his mother?

"Now there stood by the cross of Jesus his mother, and his mother's sister, Mary the wife of Cleophas, and Mary Magdalene.

"When Jesus therefore saw his mother, and the disciple standing by, whom he loved, he saith unto his mother, Woman, behold thy son!

"Then saith he to the disciple, Behold thy mother! And from that hour that disciple took her unto his own home." (John 19:25-27.)

Those kinds of feelings are not wiped away at death. Death is a harsh reality, and it does whisk loved ones from our presence without our permission, but it need not bring an eternal heartbreak. Our family feelings are eternal in nature. They were planted in you and me by a loving God who wants us to live so that we can continue forever with those family ties that bind us on earth. I believe in a loving Father in heaven who put us in family units here so that we can learn and prepare to do the same thing when we return to him. This is a practice run on what is to come if we only prepare. I bear solemn testimony to this truth!

If you can believe that, and you can, it makes a difference in how you act with your own families here. The principle of eternal family ties magnifies the importance and beauty of every moment we spend with our families. Since families can be forever, they become paramount in our lives. Feelings can and need to be expressed, love needs to be given, burdens need to be shared. Imagine — parents and teenagers getting along! With each other!

Imagine pulling into your driveway without two bicycles, the hose, a horsey on wheels and a pair of roller skates.

Imagine making a batch of cookies and ending up with enough dough to bake as many dozen as the recipe promises. Imagine having enough chocolate chips to get at least one in each cookie!

Imagine opening your desk drawer and finding a whole roll of tape *and* your good scissors right where you left them.

Imagine your bathroom floor without six wet towels, two pair of dank sneakers, three muddy socks (the mystery of the lost or extra one nagging at your mind), a pony-tail elastic, a broken mascara tube, and an assortment of sand and pebbles and twigs.

Imagine your telephone ringing and it being for you.

Imagine offering your friend a chocolate without worrying that she'll pick the one that's been nibbled on at the back and carefully replaced in its little brown paper cup.

Imagine your clothes closet without a secret cache of bananas and licorice twists and cinnamon rolls on the top shelf.

Imagine your car with a full tank of gas.

Imagine a kitchen without boots puddling on the floor, cabinets and drawers left open, fingerprints on the refrigerator, Pablum caked on the table, frozen pizza crusts crumbling on the counter, and milk rings hardening inside half a dozen glasses in the sink.

Imagine calling your ties your own.

Imagine your sofa without a beat-up blanket behind it, a slip cover over it, bread crumbs in every crevice, and a rat-tail comb between the cushions.

Imagine an evening of quiet conversation without doors slamming, radios wailing, Ping-Pong balls clacking, voices whining, feet pounding, water running, or motorcycles revving.

Imagine your birthday without a handmade card.

Imagine your table without a bouquet of battered tulips.

Imagine a clean house, a tidy yard, and a vacant toy box.

Imagine nobody calling out for you at night — or during the day.

Imagine deserted games, unused basketball hoops, forgotten merit badges gathering dust in neat rows.

Imagine dolls lined up and waiting forever on a perfectly made bed.

Imagine the sound of the clock ticking.

Imagine the silent motion of a sunbeam sliding across the floor and fading into twilight.

Imagine your home without children.

Now is the time, before our families are scattered, to enjoy our family members and make those relationships worthy of eternal duration. Give a little more love and time and appreciation to that miraculous person who is unfolding every day before your very eyes.

Let me give you my assurance that every prophet has understood and taught that families are forever. But each has also taught that for that to happen, families must prepare themselves now. That is a sobering challenge: to learn to live righteously as husbands and wives, sons and daughters; to learn not to damage with careless matters of the minute relationships that have eternal meaning.

This open letter from a father to Ann Landers, published in September 1971, is full of the kind of pain that comes from careless family relationships:

"I'm fifty-five now. I've worked hard all my life to get a house and a little business to take care of my family. But I'd give all that I own and gladly change jobs to whatever is the lowest thing I could do if only I thought my son and daughter appreciated me and loved me. It would mean more to me than anything in the whole world if they would just put their arms around me and look me in the eye and say, 'I love you, Dad, I really do.' "

It doesn't have to be like that for fathers or mothers, sons or daughters. Our homes should give us an early vision of what heaven is and will be. If we will but realize that our family unit can endure forever, and if we work unselfishly to bring that about, we can have happier homes right now and we can have eternal happiness together.

I thank my Heavenly Father for the knowledge I have that my wife and children can always be mine. I also know that *you* and *your* family can receive that same blessing if you are willing to pay the price. May a kind Heavenly Father help us to *understand* and *do*.

FATHERS — A DISAPPEARING ACT

One mother said to her little boy as his father arrived home from work, "Now, when you hear him coming, don't say, 'Oh, it's only Daddy,' even if it is only Daddy."

Obviously this father's daily homecoming did not mean too much to this little boy, and I think his case is not unusual. More and more we receive reports that the American male is so anxious to succeed as a wage-earner that he's losing sight of his most important job — that of being a parent, of making human beings human.

The father is becoming the forgotten man of our society, and without his influence in a child's life the results can be devastating. As J. Edgar Hoover once said, "The cure of crime is not the electric chair, but the high chair." Do you remember Eddie Cantor, the great comedian? He said: "Why is it men will spend more time on their stocks than their children, and it's their children in whom they have the greatest investment?"

Most fathers would tell you that they value their families above all else; but many neglect their families, failing to spend time with them or to consider their personal needs. Most such men justify their absence by claiming that it is their work that keeps them so occupied and that, after all, they work to support their families. They fail to see that that monetary support or that good example of dedication is only secondary to the personal attention that only they can give their children.

See if you recognize yourself among these examples of absent fathers:

Bill is a schoolteacher. He spends extra hours at school correcting student papers, but of course he isn't paid for it; and his small salary really has to stretch to get him through the summer months. In order to provide for his five children, Bill has a second job selling electronic equipment and sound systems at a local store. Like millions of others in the United States, Bill feels that the extra income makes up for the evenings and Saturdays away from home.

Steve is a young physician. His income, unlike Bill's, far exceeds his family's basic needs. He enjoys his large house, his airplane, his Cadillac; and the nature of his work requires that he spend long hours in his office. Frequently he leaves before his four youngsters are awake; and most evenings he arrives home sometime after 7:30, when the kids are fed and bathed and — often — already asleep. Since he sometimes works on Saturday, he takes a day off during the week when his older children are in school; usually he leaves the younger two at home on this day and plays a round of golf to get his mind off his work. Steve assumes that his wife's job is to raise the children and that his absence — whether for work or play — is justified by the money he makes.

Robert is a corporation man. He works for a national company and makes frequent moves — every two or three years — as the company requests. He could refuse to relocate, but that would jeopardize his chances for advancement. As his kids grow through their teenage years they have little chance to establish long-lasting friendships or loyalties, and often they have difficulty transferring school credits necessary for graduation. Still, these moves are essential to Robert's career, so the family makes them.

Finally there is Dick, who has no end of good deeds to do. It is not so much his career as his community spirit that keeps him away from home. Dick is very busy with his church jobs, spending two or three evenings a week and all day Sunday working there. Further, he is very active in his political party, he holds an office in the local PTA, and he coaches a Little League football team. Dick is so wrapped up in being a good example of service that he rarely sees his three children or his wife.

The excuses fathers use for being absent from their families go on and on, but none of them are good enough. In the life of each child there are opportunities for learning and loving and building reserved only for father. And if he isn't there in those special moments — if he's too busy to care — the child's very soul will be impoverished. The prophet David O. McKay once said, "No other success can compensate for failure in the home." (*Conference Reports,* April 1964.) Another prophet said, "The greatest work you'll ever do will be within the walls of your own home."

Careers may be important. The pressures outside the home may be killing. But after all, what's it all for? The buildings you build will someday crumble; the bestseller you write may yellow with age and become forgotten on some library shelf. But a child is eternal. The lessons a child learns at his father's feet will mold his life and his perceptions throughout all eternity.

Behavioral scientists tell us that the lessons not learned from fathers are having some devastating effects. They assert that the neglectful father is the root cause for many of our social headaches, including juvenile crime, drug abuse, and the counterculture rebellion against marriage and the family.

Studies show that children who have great involvement with their fathers do much better in school. They also show that children whose fathers are absent from home a great deal are more likely to be "pessimistic about the future, rate lower in responsibility and leadership, and are more likely to engage in anti-social behavior." (Lester Velie, "Where Have All the Fathers Gone?" *Reader's Digest,* April 1973, p. 157.)

So fathers — maybe all of us — need to stop that frantic pace just for a moment and look into the deep eyes of our children. How would your children answer these questions: "What's your father like? Does he love you? How does he show that love?"

One Los Angeles man thought he had found the answer to fathering. When his four-year-old daughter Melinda acquired a fixation for "The Three Little Pigs" and demanded that he read it to her night after night, the father, very pleased with his ingenuity, tape-recorded the story. When Melinda next asked for it, he simply switched on the playback. This worked for a couple of nights, but one evening Melinda pushed the storybook at her father.

"No, honey," he said, "you know how to turn on the recorder."

"Yes," said Melinda, "but I can't sit on its lap." I think it was the lap that mattered most all the time.

A friend of mine told of the relationship he had with his father as he grew up on a farm. This father loved his son in a way most of us can hardly imagine. This father and son were best friends. They worked together, they played together, and they talked together. And yet they were more than just friends, because the son respected his father in a manner that he never would have respected his peers. His father stood lower by far than the God this young man worshiped, but still his father was, in that very special way for him, next to God.

My friend remembers how he would spend great portions of time riding on this father's knee while they were on a tractor doing the farm work. Today as he considers what that must have cost in terms of a foot long since fallen asleep or of leg muscles that must have ached from the weight of a ten- or eleven-year-old son, he winces. And then he knows, in a special way, of the love his father had for him.

They talked of things that were trivial — passing things that were important only in the fancy and curiosity of a young boy. But those seemingly unimportant things led them to speak of the things that held the secrets of happiness in life. As their conversations drifted back and forth through these wonderful dimensions of friendship, the father was able to teach his son in a way that only parents are privileged to do.

And yet so many parents pass up these endless opportunities, because taking advantage of these opportunities takes time — as it did with this father and son. Hour after hour of seemingly insignificant and never-to-be-remembered discussions are gently sprinkled with the treasures of life and eternity.

I've always thought it significant that God himself, whose brilliant mind penetrates every mystery of the universe, whose abilities are so keen that he fashions worlds, chooses to be called by the simple name "Father."

So fathers, if you want a legacy that lasts, look for it in your sons' abilities to square their shoulders to accept new responsibility, in your daughters' soft compassionate eyes. You're not an advertising man, nor a merchant, nor a trucker, nor a doctor; you're first a father. It's a job that promises endless joy, an eternal calling. Make time for it and thank God that he too is a father who takes time to care!

SIX STEPS TO
FAMILY SECURITY

One of life's greatest stresses for most of us, especially during days of runaway inflation, is providing for ourselves. Who hasn't known panic in the supermarket as he has watched four bags of groceries mount to fifty or sixty dollars? Who hasn't wondered if he could afford to fill his gas tank or pay the bill that just arrived?

I've often thought that the reason most Americans become so hysterical when they win money on game shows is because most of the time they feel desperately insecure. You probably know the feeling. You think, "Oh, if I could just find a way to get ahead."

One young lady I know wanted so desperately to win some money that she decided to enter a contest advertised on the back of a cereal box. The object was to create as many words as possible from the individual letters in the product's commercial slogan. She pored over an unabridged dictionary, checking every word on every page until she had found over ten thousand words that contained the necessary letters. As far as I know, she still didn't win, but what an effort she was willing to expend just for the chance of winning an unexpected sum of money.

What's your method to find family security — or, as the saying goes, keep the wolf from the door?

One attempt to find security is illustrated in this modern version of a well-known fable.

Once upon a time there lived in a country field an industrious little ant and a lazy grasshopper. Early in the spring the ant began house cleaning, giving his old furniture and clothing to the Goodwill and repairing all winter's damage to his house as he worked. On his way back from a trip to the dump, he passed the grasshopper lounging on a warm rock.

"Hey, fella, what's your rush?" the grasshopper asked.

"I've got work to do to keep my house up and get ready for next winter," the ant replied. "It wouldn't hurt you to make some preparations yourself."

"No way!" answered the grasshopper." I've got to work on my tan and improve my tennis game. Winter's a long way off."

"Nevertheless..." warned the ant, and he went on his way.

By the time summer was fully warm, the little ant had his pantry organized and had started laying in supplies for the winter. Every morning he was up early, and all day he labored at finding and storing food. One day as he struggled home under the weight of a huge bread crumb, he came upon the grasshopper sitting on the rock playing his fiddle.

"Brother," said the grasshopper, "I don't see how you do it."

"I don't see any way not to," responded the ant. "If I want to eat next winter I've got to provide for it now. Why don't you get busy yourself?"

"Well," yawned the grasshopper, "I just can't get into that. Besides, it's fishing season and I've got a terrific novel to finish reading as well. Winter's a long way off."

"Nevertheless..." warned the ant, and he went on his way.

September found the little ant dragging firewood and scraps of coal home to burn as fuel in the winter. Carefully he packed it away in his basement, and all day long he carried and organized and stored. Late one afternoon he passed the grasshopper lying on the rock sipping lemonade and wearing sunglasses.

"Last chance to catch some rays," the grasshopper commented.

"You can't keep warm in January on summer's sunburn," the ant said just a little irritably. "Haven't you done *anything* about taking care of yourself next winter?"

"Something will turn up," the grasshopper responded languidly. "I just can't worry about January in all this sunshine."

"Nevertheless..." warned the ant, and he went on his way.

The first snow fell in early October, and by the end of the month the little ant's home was up to the windows in drifts. Snug by a warm fire, he was enjoying his evening meal when there was a knock at the door. He opened it, and in blew the grasshopper dressed in rags and shivering with the cold. Close behind him came the county welfare agent, a beetle of considerable importance.

"See?" said the ant to the grasshopper, "I told you winter would catch up with you."

"Good evening," said the beetle while the grasshopper's teeth chattered. "Since you worked so hard all summer and you have so much here," (he looked around and made mental notes of supplies)"the county is assigning to you the support of this citizen."

In a moment the beetle was gone, and the grasshopper was warming himself by the fire and finishing the ant's supper.

"See?" he said between bites, "I told you something would turn up. And soon it will be spring again."

"Nevertheless," sighed the ant, and he stared out the window.

In this modernized fable the grasshopper thought he had found the sure way to security. He simply passed the responsibility to someone else. "Take care of me," he insisted. And his method is typical of many in our society who refuse to accept responsibility for themselves.

You've seen it. Some learn to trust their credit cards, believing their plastic plates to be an unending source for consumer goods. As one wife said to her husband, "So what if we're out of money? We've still got our credit cards."

Others expect society to take care of them. They believe the government is a pocketbook that never dries up. By 1976, for example, over 16.7 million people were on government welfare and were thus looking to someone else to take care of them. ("Welfare Mess: Any Hope of Solution?" *U. S. News and World Report,* June 7, 1976, p. 33.)

But none of us really wants to forfeit responsibility for himself. We know that passing our family security on to anybody else is the ultimate form of insecurity.

In the United States we have a tradition of independence to uphold. It was their individual strength and faith in self that gave our Founding Fathers the power to declare this an independent nation, and it is the same individual sense of self-reliance that maintains our personal liberty. No man feels really free if he must look to someone else for daily support. It is fine to help your brother — and to receive help from him — but each must help the other to stand alone, not to lean. Freedom implies the ability to choose one's own way, and no man can have that or the self-respect that goes with it if he constantly requires someone else's support.

All of us want to be self-dependent, but how do we manage it when our dollars just don't seem to stretch far enough? Consider these six steps toward family security, these six ways to help yourself be individually independent.

First, each person should select a suitable vocation or profession and pursue the training needed to become skillful in it. Each of us needs to have a skill he can sell in the marketplace. Not only does this apply to adults, but also to the youth. Those of us who are parents have a duty to see to it that our children receive counsel to help them select careers that will meet their personal needs. We must sit down with them and discover their dreams, nurture their talents. In a world where potential and talent are passed out in such abundance, no one should be insecure because he doesn't have a marketable skill.

The second step toward family security is to be well-educated. The prepared person reads, writes, and does basic mathematics. He takes advantage of local resources and studies good books. He understands current events and is aware of the social and political ideas that shape his life. He understands how to be a good citizen and how to have his individual voice make some impact on the world he lives in.

A third step to family security is to learn proper management of money. Our resources are just not infinitely expandable, no matter how much we wish they were. If you consistently spend more than you make, you're in trouble. Don't fall into the trap of purchasing things that you really can't pay for. Even if you delay your payments for another day, your payments will eventually fall due, and it will hurt just as much then as it does now. Instead, make financial goals and save during times of production for times of nonproduction.

The fourth step to family security is to provide as much as possible for your family through gardening, sewing, and producing household items. Not only does this usually save you money, but it prepares every member with the basic skills that will always serve him well. Where legally permitted, it is wise to store a year's supply of food so you will not go hungry in the case of personal disaster.

The fifth step to family security is to take active measures to stay in good health. We are hearing much about preventive medicine, especially from insurance companies who know how expensive medical payments are. To keep your family healthy, work together on practicing sound nutrition, physical fitness, and weight control. Join the joggers or the jump-ropers or the yoga fans, and stay in shape. Do not indulge in alcohol or tobacco: both can debilitate a body that was meant to be healthy. For your family's security, you just can't afford it.

The last step to family security is to build for yourself an inner strength that will not collapse under the least stress. In all of our lives there is challenge. It may be financial; it may not. But whatever its origin, and however much it hurts, we must learn to face challenge with the confidence and stability that is born of a daily communication with the Lord. When we have learned through personal prayer that the Lord really loves us — that he knows us intimately and that he is aware of our needs — we can face with courage whatever the world chooses to throw at us. Knowing that the Lord loves us and trusts us and expects us not to be defeated nobodies is the final security in an otherwise insecure world.

THE GREAT TURN-ON —
YOUR CHILDREN AND TV

If you've ever wondered just how much influence television has on the behavior of children, consider this incident reported in the *Wall Street Journal*. An elementary school was having some kind of a diagnostic spelling test to see how well the children could spell. At one point the teacher said, "Tell me how to spell 'relief.'" And the great majority of the students responded, "R-O-L-A-I-D-S!"

There's no doubt that television is here to stay in our culture and that it influences our behavior and thought and speech in more ways than we imagine. A survey done by the Center for Family Research, for instance, revealed that more children between the ages of six and eight could identify television personalities Donny and Marie Osmond than could identify Jimmy Carter. Even among mid-adolescents, ages fifteen to seventeen, only one in four recognize Anwar Sadat. Nearly two-fifths of those in that blissful age don't know what inflation is, but 84 percent can identify Donny and Marie, thanks to television.

If children are learning a new way to spell *relief* that defies pho-netics, and if Donny and Marie are as familiar to them as are the neighbors next door, I can't help but wonder what else all of us are picking up from television that changes our behavior and attitudes in ways we don't even suppose. Are we being conditioned to new and sometimes unacceptable norms of behavior by the hours and hours of television we allow into our private environment? And what about our children, those avid television watchers? What's happening to them?

Here's one example. In a 1976 report to the people of Canada, the Royal Commission on Violence in the Communications Industry concluded that media violence can lead to an increase in a person's level of aggression.

The Commission further commented: "There seems to be a rapidly expanding dossier of crimes which have been copied from media presentations. In California, a seventy-one-year-old man tried to rob a bank with a toy gun because he had seen it done on TV and it looked so easy. In Alberta, a youth hanged himself trying to copy a mock hanging performed by rock star Alice Cooper in his television act. Television dramas describing extortion attempts based on planting a pressure-sensitive bomb on an airplane led to an outbreak of real extortion attempts based on this threat. After the media coverage of Evel Knievel's various jumps, a rash of injuries resulted from children's attempts to copy his actions. In other words modeling or imitative learning does affect children's behavior, and can instigate antisocial or self destructive acts. " (Glen C. Griffin and Victor B. Cline, "Screening Out the Garbage: How to Teach 'Correct Principles' About Television in the Home," *Ensign,* August 1976, p. 20.)

In a different study, a Stanford psychologist Albert Bandura studied five groups of nursery school children and how they responded after observing certain things. The first group observed adults behaving aggressively toward a plastic doll. The second group saw a film of the same thing. The third group saw a cartoon cat enacting the same aggressive acts on the poor doll. The other two groups of children were control groups: one control group was exposed to a nonaggressive, nonviolent film, and the other control group saw no film or models at all.

The children in all of the groups were then exposed to mild frustration, and they were put one by one into a room with the same plastic doll. Each child's behavior and responses toward the doll were then observed and recorded.

The researchers discovered two frightening things as they watched the children work out their frustrations in the room with the doll. First, exposure to aggressive films or models taught the children new and novel ways to be aggressive themselves. They, in fact, imitated the unique, assaultive behavior they had previously seen in the films. Second, once the children had seen others perform aggressive acts toward the doll, their own inhibitions against violence were reduced, and they felt freer to spank or shoot the doll or do whatever occurred to them. (Griffin and Cline, p. 20.)

Each of us learns best, after all, by imitation. The same parents who laughed wholeheartedly at their three-year-old when she said, "I used to be flat — now I'm fluffy," probably would not think it was so funny if she later imitated and adopted the sexual immorality of characters portrayed on some programs or the value systems of others.

It's time we recognize that a steady diet of television has a powerful influence in our lives. If it can gradually brainwash us to think that only one kind of toothpaste can save us from tooth decay or that only one kind of soap gives us shiny floors, television's power to shape our behavior is overwhelming.

So what are you going to do about it? Is the answer to chop down your antenna or sell your television at the next garage sale? For most of us, that probably isn't the best answer. Television can bring wonders into our homes. History comes alive before our eyes; we visit countries we may never hope to see; we explore the marvels of science depicted by a human cell or a star a million miles away. Most of us aren't willing to give that up.

But there is an answer that lies somewhere between giving up the television and mindlessly watching it for hours until all family conversation is dulled and until life is scheduled according to what can be done during commercials. That answer consists of setting guidelines for television viewing — guidelines worked out by the whole family.

Let me share with you ten guidelines established by pediatrician Glen C. Griffin and internationally recognized writer and psychologist Victor B. Cline. These rules work for their families, and maybe they can work for yours.

"1. Unless there is something really worthwhile 'ON,' the TV will be 'OFF.' " TV will not be used merely as a way to fritter away time when there is nothing else to do.

"2. If a program does not meet gospel standards for children, it is not appropriate for parents either.

"3. Parents won't use the TV as a babysitter to get the kids out of the way.

"4. Certain types of programs do not justify watching at all, such as those that are immoral or promote violence.

"5. Children's shows will be checked frequently by parents, because not all children's educational programs meet gospel standards. Is poor or insulting language used? Is there hitting, shouting, or disruption? Are characters and situations likely to lead to nightmares? Are inappropriate materials discussed or shown? Are gospel principles compromised? If so, then that program is not turned on — even if it has widespread acclaim.

"6. Selected sports events are viewed in moderation.

"7. When a particularly excellent television special is scheduled, it should be put on the family calendar so that the family can enjoy it together.

"8. On the Sabbath, if the television is turned on at all, the program must be in keeping with the Sabbath Day.

"9. Programs are reviewed in family night before being scheduled.

"10. The house must be tidy and schoolwork done or under control before the television is turned on." (Griffin and Cline, p. 21.)

Those guidelines work for some families. Can you find television-viewing guidelines that can work for you? When you first turn off the television, you may notice the silence. But when you begin to see chores being done, family members actually talking to one another, and good books opened, you'll think that silence is golden.

The author of Proverbs reminds us that if you will train up a child in the way he ought to go, he will not depart from your teachings when he is old.

PART THREE

THE BREADTH
OF BROTHERHOOD

LET YOUR
FEELINGS SHOW

I remember hearing about presidential candidate Adlai Stevenson who liked to appeal to the voters through their children. Quite often during his campaign speeches he would ask how many children would like to be candidates for the Presidency of the United States. Dozens of hands would be raised. Then, instead of going on about opportunity, he would bring down the house by asking how many candidates would like to be kids again and stretching his own hand as high as possible.

Can you think back through the mist of time and thought to your years of childhood? For most of us — as for the late Adlai Stevenson — childhood seems like a golden yesterday when the world seemed larger, more expansive, more hopeful; when ice cream was colder and holidays were more enticing; when every day and every event had a sweeter cutting edge.

But a funny thing happens to us as we grow up. We learn to "play it cool"; an emotional ice age sets in. We learn to somehow feel embarrassed or ashamed to show joy, fear, pity, or longing. We first start by hiding our feelings, and then, with the petrifying action of time, we learn not to have feelings at all.

I met a friend one beautiful April morning and remarked, "Spring in the air, Bill."

"If you insist," was my friend's reply, at which he jumped into the air, tipped his hat, and sauntered happily down the street.

Do you ever feel that glad to be alive, like you have soda in your veins? Do you sometimes have moments of spontaneous joy, or moments of spontaneous compassion for another human being? Sometimes we say with a touch of shame, "Excuse me, my feelings got the better of me." But how sad for all of us if we become so robot-like that we have no feelings at all welling up from the depths of our personality.

John Ruskin once wrote, "The ennobling difference between one man and another is that one feels more than another." Those words are true through the gamut of life — all the way from how we feel about our neighbor to how we respond to a Beethoven symphony.

A famous soprano was once asked to evaluate two young women auditioning for the Metropolitan Opera. She explained her preference by indicating that one of the singers shared much more of herself with her audience. While this young singer did not have an extraordinary voice, she was chosen because she did have a remarkable ability to convey emotion.

All of us can give more to life if we recognize the wisdom in feelings. The secret of getting along with people is recognizing the feelings behind whatever mask they happen to put on.

When a child at home or at school acts unruly, discourteous, or downright rude, it may be his way of saying, "My feelings are hurt. You don't pay attention to me."

If a husband or wife is neglectful or grouchy, it may be his or her way of saying, "I'm sad. Nothing is going right for me."

When we say of someone, "He understands me," we're really saying, "He knows how I feel."

A bright young woman with a degree in merchandising landed her first job at an exclusive department store in her home town. The manager was near retirement, and he gave her complete control of her own department: she was to handle displays, purchases, employees, the works. Enthusiastic about the opportunity and confident in her employer's trust, she set about making some drastic changes which she was sure would improve the department.

Much to her disappointment, the manager disapproved of her very first ideas. As the weeks passed, he found fault with her every move — from far-reaching plans to simple merchandise displays.

Frustrated and angry, she poured out her confusion to her father. Her dad thought a few minutes and then explained that while he couldn't give her advice about merchandising, he could see another problem. He suggested that the manager might be expressing not her failure so much as his own fears of being replaced.

The young woman returned to work determined to be sensitive to her employer's feelings, and there developed between them a relationship in which she learned a great deal from his experience, and both felt happy and productive.

Just as the off-key singing of a tone-deaf child may not tell you anything of the symphonies in her heart, so another's actions or words may not always tell you what his feelings are. Want to get along with other people? Then learn to recognize how they feel and let them know you recognize those feelings.

When you let another's feelings speak to you and when you in turn let your own feelings answer back, you instinctively know what to do in any situation. One afternoon in early spring, a group of school children made their way home together, carefully skirting puddles of rainwater left from the morning's storm. Suddenly one little girl stopped, and the tears welled up in her eyes as she looked down at the mud oozing up around her brand new Keds in a deep puddle she had not seen.

Immediately the girl walking beside her stepped right into that puddle, face to face with her friend. The two of them laughed together at the squishing their feet made as they drew them out of the mud and within a few minutes the whole group were laughing and shouting to one another as they stomped and splashed their way down the road.

Feelings: it takes courage to show them in a world where the seeming ideal is never to be shocked, surprised, or deeply moved. Feelings: it takes insight to read them in others behind whatever behavior those others show.

A story is told of a little woman who understood the feelings of a man in her neighborhood who was large and powerfully built, but who had a child's mind. This woman often called on the fellow to help her by working in her yard or carrying groceries from the market.

One day as she returned from town, she saw a crowd gathered in the schoolyard. At the center of the crowd stood this man, a ball bat in his hands and two youngsters who had taunted him cowering before him. The police had been called and were threatening the man with their guns. He had not moved or responded to them in any way. The little woman made her way through the crowd and approached her friend, asking him to help her get her packages home. Relieved of his fear and humiliation, he dropped the bat, gathered up her bundles, and walked quietly away with her.

Feelings make us very vulnerable to one another, and often it seems safer to hide our feelings or to stifle them before they fully develop. Doing this can spare us the awkwardness of having said too much too strongly, the disillusionment of having tried and failed, the pain of having hoped for and not realized our goals. But this no-risk behavior, this avoidance of commitment, also leads to frequent job changes, divorce, and shifts in religious or political allegiance. In short, it is a shallow way to live. If you could eliminate emotion and enthusiasm from your work, your education, your marriage, your beliefs, and your friendships, would any of these be of real value anymore? It is our genuine feelings about one another and about our experiences that make life rich.

FRIENDSHIP — LIFE'S GOLD

We live in a transient society. In fact, being able to pack boxes to move has become one of life's more essential skills. When you learn to drive a car, you'd better learn to drive a moving van, too, because chances are you'll be moving five or six times or more during your adult life.

All this moving around can be adventurous, but it has its pitfalls, too. We are gradually becoming a society where people no longer know their closest neighbors. People can live next door in high-rise apartments and not know whose shaver they can hear buzzing through the wall. In one suburban neighborhood a man was looking for the home of an elderly lady, and her neighbors across the street said they'd never heard of her.

The latest symbol of friendship, in fact, is the ad series for the telephone companies, showing one friend moving away from another. And those in big cities find that most of the people they encounter every day are strangers. They move in an anonymous world.

But with all this flux, most of us still have old-fashioned hearts. We yearn for true, stable, lifelong friendship. We think with nostalgia about those days when friends were together for life, when they raised each other's barns and quilted each other's bedding. The "here today, gone tomorrow" relationships in life just don't seem to be enough. Instant popularity or passing acquaintance is no substitute for a real friend.

To the rich, fully realized life, friendship is like gold. It is not valuable for something else. It is valuable for itself.

C. Raymond Beran said about friendship: "What is a friend? I will tell you. It is a person with whom you dare to be yourself. Your soul can be naked with him. He seems to ask of you to put on nothing, only to be what you are. He does not want you to be better or worse. When you are with him, you feel as a prisoner feels who has been declared innocent. You do not have to be on your guard. You can say what you think, so long as it is genuinely you. He understands those contradictions in your nature that lead others to misjudge you. With him you breathe freely... he understands. You can weep with him... laugh with him, pray with him. Through it all — and underneath — he sees and knows and loves you." (Ray C. Beran, in Susan Polis Schutz., ed., "A Lifetime of Friendship," 1978 calendar.)

Sounds good, doesn't it? We'd all like to have that kind of friend. In this sense of the word, can you call your neighbor a friend? Can you call your spouse a friend? Can you call your God a friend? We've heard it so much it sounds commonplace, but it was Ralph Waldo Emerson who said, "The only way to have [that kind of] friend is to be one."

A Greek myth adapted by Jewel Varnado illustrates enduring friendship:

"Darkness filled the corners of the dungeon under the castle. All about on the hard floor lay men who had been arrested by the ruler's soldiers. Most of them had been condemned to death. A hopeless silence filled the room so that the low words of the young man outside the barred door sounded loud and angry.

" 'What did you do, my good friend, Pythias?' the young man demanded. 'What did you do that so displeased the king?'

"The prisoner at the door sighed. His hand reached through the narrow bars and touched his friend's arm. Since early childhood these two had always been together. Now Pythias knew that he was going to leave his friend forever and his heart ached at the thought of this separation.

" 'I did nothing, Damon,' he insisted, 'but the King has claimed that I am a rebel. There is nothing that can be done about it.'

" 'Then what can I do for you?' Damon asked. 'Shall I go to your home and comfort your parents?'

"Neither of the young men had heard the great outer door open. They did not see the ruler as he came near to them.

" 'I would like to see them myself once more,' Pythias' voice was hopeless. 'I would come back here and pay with my life if I could only say farewell to them.'

"A loud laugh startled the two young men. Damon whirled and found himself face to face with his king. Quickly he bowed and waited for the ruler to speak. Again, the king laughed as he looked at the prisoner.

" 'So you would come back to die if I would let you go to your distant home?' he mocked Pythias and all the prisoners.

" 'I would come back,' Pythias stated simply. 'I promise.'

" 'How do I know that you would keep your promise?' the king's eyes narrowed as he watched the man. 'You are trying to cheat me. You cannot go.'

" 'Then let me stay in prison in his place,' Damon looked straight at the king as he made his request. 'He has never broken a promise, but if he does not return, I will die for him on the day that is set for his execution.'

"The king was amused. This strange request would make a delightful story to tell his friends. A young man who offered to die for his friend! This was the best jest of the year and he and his courtiers would watch it with interest.

"Soon the prison door closed behind Damon, and Pythias was on his way home. The days passed and the day of execution came nearer and nearer. Day by day the king came to the prison to taunt the foolish young man. Again and again his cruel laughter rang out.

" 'If Pythias does not come back, it will not be his fault,' Damon stated calmly. 'Something will have happened to him.'

"At last the day for the execution arrived and Pythias had not returned. The king and his courtiers jeered at Damon as he was led from the cell.

" 'The man who dies for his friend, a false friend,' they called out. 'We told you that he would not return.'

" 'He will come if he can,' Damon said to himself as he walked straight and tall in the line of condemned men. 'He will come if —'

" 'Here he comes! Here he comes!' a soldier ran shouting to the king.

"Damon smiled as he saw his friend. Pythias was hardly able to breathe. Storms and misfortunes had beset him all the way back. He had feared that Damon would die before he could arrive. His face beamed with happiness when he found his friend alive. Quickly he fell into the line of prisoners and pushed Damon aside.

" 'I came,' he panted.

" 'I knew that you would!'

"The king could hardly believe his eyes and ears. Never had he known that there could be such friendship. His heart softened before such a great love.

" 'Go!' he said to the two young men. 'Go back to your homes.'

"Then he turned to his stunned courtiers and added, 'I would give all my wealth to have one such friend.' " (Stan and Sharon Miller, *Especially for Mormons,* vol. 3 [Provo, Utah: Kellirae Arts, 1976], pp. 129-31.)

Each of us treads his mortal path alone. No one else shares the whole of our experience. The joys and pains are in many ways ours alone. But to find a friend along the walk is life's greatest treasure, its most enduring gift. And to find that friend we must first be one — willing to sacrifice our time, our prejudices, even our life.

It was our Lord who said, "Greater love hath no man than this, that a man lay down his life for his friends." (John 15:13.)

In this world of hurried acquaintances and passing nods, find yourself a friend, someone whose heart beats in rhythm with yours. You'll find in such a companionship not only your greatest joy but your greatest growth.

FAMILY PRIDE

Have you ever wondered what your children are going to remember about their growing-up years? Will they remember mainly that you were always in a hurry and didn't have time to listen? Will they remember mainly that the house was clean and they were chided to keep it that way? Just what will they be, those "golden" memories of childhood?

I remember hearing a story about a family who desperately wanted to redo their bathroom — or at least the parents did. The tub was an old-fashioned one that stood on legs; the wallpaper seemed faded. But every year they drained their savings account — not to redo the old bathroom, but to go on a couple of family skiing trips. Thinking about those trips, the dad says, "Our oldest boy is in the army now, and he often mentions in his letters what a great time we had on those trips. You know, I can't imagine his writing home, 'Boy, we really have a swell bathroom, haven't we?' " (Stan and Sharon Miller, *Especially for Mormons*, vol. 3 [Provo, Utah: Kellirae Arts, 1976], p. 103.)

Your children aren't going to remember how much money you spent on them or whether their house was the fanciest one on the block. No, in this world where each of us can just be another face in the crowd, another seat in the stadium, what your children will remember is the sense of belonging to something great — a sense of heritage, a sense of family that in this world gives them a unique identity.

I remember when I was a nineteen-year-old soldier fighting in World War II. I didn't want to be there; I'd rather have been home playing baseball. I remember a statement Ernie Pyle, the great war correspondent, made during the war: "If you are to win, you have to have confidence in your leader and pride in your outfit." Pride in your outfit — sometimes that's all that pulled us through the misery that was all around us. Pride in *their* outfit — maybe that will be the only thing that will pull your children through as the challenges of the world surround them.

I once asked a gracious young woman how she had become what she was, how she had lived through childhood and adolescence with such undeviating sweetness and self-mastery, avoiding youth's typical pitfalls. Her answer was telling: "I knew my parents loved me, and I didn't ever want to hurt them."

My father said it this way: "A good name is better than a girdle of gold. Remember, I gave you a good name."

That's pride in your outfit. You see that kind of thing at work when alumni from a college gather for a class reunion. They sing the school song and praise the football team. They retell for the hundredth time the antics of the senior class president, and they genuinely believe that there was no other group quite like them in the world. I remember seeing at a Harvard University graduation a man so old and feeble he could hardly totter across the lawn to a group of folding chairs. And do you know what he had on his straw hat, written across the red band for all to see? "Harvard-02." He wasn't going to miss his class reunion. That's pride in your outfit.

How are you going to help your family develop this kind of family pride, this sense of belonging one to another that transcends all the forces that pull people apart? How are you going to teach your children that they have a heritage to live up to, a reason to be somebodies?

One young man told this story: "Until I was fifteen years old I kind of prided myself in being a model loser. No matter what kind of competition, I always lost better than anyone else did. People often mentioned what a great sport I was. Deep down I got to thinkin' maybe I was supposed to be a loser.

"And then one day my Grandpa Fitzpatrick came to a track meet and watched me run and lose and do all those gracious things that 'good sports' do... and after the meet he told me a story about his dad, who was Ireland's distance running champion.

"Great-grandpa Fitz said that every time he ran in competition he felt like he was running for the whole Fitzpatrick family, and that all the greatness of the family was running in his blood, and that he was special.... 'Fitzpatricks,' he said, 'came to earth because the angels got tired of losing to them.'

"I laughed, and then Grandpa said, 'You've got a lot of your great-grandpa's natural talent... I'll bet you've got a lot of his pride, too!'

"You know, after that day I ran harder than I've ever run, and I started winning, too.

"Sometimes when you find out where you came from, you find out who you are." (Michael McLean.)

When they run, your kids will run better and farther and faster if they know they're running for the whole clan. Give them pride in being a Jensen or a Greer or a Jones, in belonging to your family, to each other and nobody else. Here are some ways to begin.

Teach your kids about their grandparents and great-grandparents and Uncle Fred. They need to know that they had a great-grandmother who had the strength to rear four children alone in a primitive cabin when her pioneer husband was killed. They need to hear about the grandfather who immigrated on a boat just to carve out a better life for his family.

I asked one young boy named Peter where he got his name. His answer? "From the Bible." *Oh, no!* I wanted to shout to him. Your parents named you for your great-grandfather, an English teacher who stood six-feet-four and straight as a stick, who had a voice so feeling and resonant that when he read Shakespeare his students never forgot. But Peter's parents hadn't bothered to tell him that, so he thought he had gotten his name only from the Bible.

Your own ancestors are just as compelling, just as courageous. Share them with your children. Let your children know that the will to live fully, the daring to face life head-on with strength and compassion, runs right down to their genes.

Here's another way to build family pride and spirit. Consciously build into your lives family traditions that pull your hearts and memories together long after distance has separated you. Traditions may vary. In some families, it may be a dilapidated but magical ornament that dad puts on the top of the tree every year at Christmastime. It may be a jack-o-lantern carving contest at Halloween or some songs that the family always sings when they're together in the car. One family I know leaves a small bouquet of flowers in a little vase by the dinner plate of a child who has shown some special kindness or who has mastered some new task. It's just a way of saying, "We noticed." In another family, the mother invented a fanciful series of stories about a squirrel and told them to each child at bedtime. The children — now all adults — say that whenever they see a squirrel, they are reminded again of their mother's love for them and of the warm sharing times together. Traditions? The possibilities are endless, bounded only by your imagination.

When you look around and see the world as a frightening place to rear children, full of lures and disappointments and temptations, remember that just as pride in the outfit has saved more than one soldier and has made him a victor, so will pride in the family save your children. When the whole world is searching desperately for identity, your children will have a sense of belonging, a sense of themselves. When their peers experiment wildly, trying to solve old problems with new solutions, your children will confide in you. When all others fall just before the race is completed or the standard is met, your children will keep running and keep trying because they know they represent their whole family. That's pride in your outfit!

FIRST THINGS FIRST?

Get away from the city lights sometime soon and take a look up at that monumental darkness that extends billions of miles into space. Scientists have discovered in outer space some 7×10^{13} stars. How many is that? Well, if each were a single piece of paper, stood up and pressed flat against the next, the stars — all 7×10^{13} of them — would stretch around the world six hundred times.

We know that many of those stars have planets that revolve around them; we know that among all those stars, our own sun is very small — insignificant in the vast scheme of things. We know that each of us is just a small speck on a small planet.

What in all that universe of mystery and marvel is most important?

One clear, soft autumn evening that question was asked as a father and his daughter took a walk beneath the lofty elms that graced their street. People had always said they could see a certain magic between this father and his daughter. Even when she had been just a toddler and he had been just a graduate student, there had been an open, visible, two-way pride between them. So, that night she slipped her hand into his, and with complete trust that the answer would be right, she asked, "Daddy . . . what is the most important thing of all?"

"What is the most important thing of all?" It is a silly question in a way, but a profound one in another way. It was a night for questions like that, and so the father thought about the question as they walked for several silent minutes, and then he gave his daughter the correct answer in just one word: "Relationships."

The thought had never before come to him quite like that, and yet, as he said it, he knew it was inspired and he formulated questions to teach his daughter what he felt.

"Can you think of a single better measurement of happiness than the number and depth of the relationships a person has?"

The moonlight caught her hair as she answered. "Certainly not money . . . not possessions . . . maybe testimony and conviction that God lives. . . ." she said, "but that is a relationship, isn't it . . . with God?"

The father nodded, then went on teaching himself as he taught her: "Can't almost everything be translated into a relationship . . . our problems, our fulfillments, our concerns and worries, our joys and pleasures . . . don't all stem from one relationship or another . . . and if they do, why don't we focus more effort on relationships?" (Paul H. Dunn and Richard M. Eyre, *Relationships . . . Self . . . Family . . . God* [Salt Lake City: Bookcraft, Inc., 1974], pp. 1-5.)

That girl's answer to her father on that evening seems true for all of us. We don't focus more effort on relationships because we are all working so hard on achievement, on getting things done, and on gaining material things. That word is really the villain, isn't it? *Things* — things are the antithesis of people and they form the basis for choices we face so often: people or things, relationships or achievements, taking time to get to know someone or getting another thing done.

One writer said that "things get in the saddle and ride mankind." And most of us feel bridled and at a gallop most of the time under that pressure. *Things.* Why is it that we usually choose the thing over the person, even when we know that the thing is temporary and the person is forever? Why do so many of us view relationships as a means to an end, and not an end in themselves?

We're guilty of looking at people and even at God with the same kinds of eyes that enterprising advertisers used to look at cows along the railroad line in England. They put coats stitched with ads on these cows, who were grazing at the side of the London-Brighton railroad line. These days even a cow can't exist for its own sake.

We're not much different than these ad men in our relationships with people. We ask ourselves, "What can he or she do for me?" And if we come up dry, we don't waste any time on that relationship. Too often, our relationships have an ulterior motive of achieving some objective, some *thing* other than the relationship itself.

The old expression, "First *things* first," has permeated our hearts — and things come first in our lives — too often, things come before our families, our friends, or our Father in heaven.

One day I happened to say to a friend, "Who are you?" He gave me some forty-eight correct answers. Among them were: a father, a child, a husband, an accountant, a Jaycee, a basement remodeler, a friend, a fisherman, a football fan, a child of God, a part-time real estate salesman, an investor. His list went on and on.

Then I asked my friend, "Which five of your self-definitions are the most important?" It was easy to choose, he said: a child of God, a father, a husband, a child of his parents, a friend.

Then I asked him the stinger. "On which five of your forty-eight self-definitions do you spend the most time and the most mental energy?" The answer to this question was easy, too, but not pleasant. He admitted that he gave most of his time and energy to being an accountant, a basement remodeler, a Jaycee, a salesman, and a football fan. (He had to add football fan because he added up the football hours from the week, and the total was greater than those he had spent with his children.)

He noticed, and so did I, that his list of time expenditures was primarily oriented to *things*, not people. Are we any different? Play the same game with yourself and find out.

In our hurry-up world where the most successful among us seem to be those who get the most done, we can find ourselves becoming more and more task-oriented. Every day is full of lists of things we must do, and woe to the people who get in our way.

What would have happened to the injured man along the road if the Good Samaritan had been so involved with his list of pressing errands that he hadn't looked up?

Task-oriented. What a far cry that is from being people-oriented! One mother said that she had tried for three days to get her teenage son to do several jobs around the house. Finally she wrote him a note, listing the chores; she signed it, "Love, Mother."

When she arrived home from work that night, her son put his arms around her neck and kissed her. Then he picked up the note and crossed "Love, Mother" off the list. Nothing else on the list had been accomplished, but she didn't mind a bit.

Relationships. I'm not suggesting that your entire life come to a halt, but I am saying that there is no place as meaningful for a life's investment than in the hearts of your friends, your family, your God. Everything else dims with time, but people are eternal.

A man whose life was consumed in his garden and yard lived on a street near ours. Not a weed was ever allowed to trespass into his grass. Not a branch was ever allowed to grow beyond the careful trim. He could be seen out in his yard working almost any hour of the day. I applaud his high standards. But did he ever share his gardening know-how, his vegetables, or his flowers with his neighbors? No. He couldn't be bothered. When he was invited to neighborhood parties or barbecues, he made it known that he didn't care for people and wouldn't come. When a little girl's pet rabbit strayed into his yard, he killed it, worried that it would destroy some precious corner of his lot.

And though his flowers blossomed bountifully, he became a withered spirit, dried up with irritabilities. Nobody noticed when he died and his yard was left to be overcome with weeds.

The relationships you have with yourself, your fellowmen, your family, and your God are not the perimeter of your life — they are your life's very soul. Nothing in this wide universe compares. The hours of your life are ticking away. Are you spending them on people or on things?

"UNTO THE LEAST . . ."

Christmas is the season of holly, mistletoe, and counting how many shopping days are left before your bank balance reads zero. Everyone loves the gifts, the surprises, the Christmas secrets whispered behind closed doors. But do you ever find yourself, like me, wishing there was some gift you could give to the Lord? Do you wish you could be like the wise men and carry some treasure of special worth into his very presence?

The Lord has given us everything, even our very breath, the life power that sustains every moment of our existence. But what can we do for him? He has given us commandments and asked us to obey them. But those commandments are given for our *own* good. They are given to strengthen *us*, to make *us* better and happier. The only thing we really do for him, in the final analysis, is to give our love to his children here and to bless and uplift and encourage those souls we meet and live with every day. Every one of them, after all, bears the stamp of his divine parentage.

In Matthew we read of the love Christ expects us to show others. On the day of judgment the Lord will say this to those who have pleased him:

"For I was an hungred, and ye gave me meat: I was thirsty, and ye gave me drink: I was a stranger, and ye took me in:

"Naked, and ye clothed me: I was sick, and ye visited me: I was in prison, and ye came unto me.

"Then shall the righteous answer him, saying, Lord, when saw we thee an hungred, and fed thee? or thirsty, and gave thee drink?

"When saw we thee a stranger, and took thee in? or naked, and clothed thee?"

And Jesus answered that classic question with this: "Verily I say unto you, Inasmuch as ye have done it unto one of the least of these my brethren, ye have done it unto me." (Matthew 25:35-37, 40.)

We live in a world where high achievement is lauded; we work to develop talents and knowledge; we chase wealth and fame and honor. But all these things mean nothing if we do not develop the highest gift of all — a grand capacity to love our fellows, to hurt when they hurt, to anticipate and meet their unspoken needs.

It is easy, perhaps, to love those we admire. But the truly great soul is he who serves someone who can do nothing for him. As Henry Higgins says to Eliza in *My Fair Lady*, "The greatest secret, Eliza . . . is in having the same manners for all human souls; in short, behaving as though you were in heaven, where there are no third-class carriages, and one soul is as good as another."

Do you give your love in service and sensitivity to the stranger, the less powerful, the poor, the unimportant, the child? A story I heard tells of a boy who missed his chance to love someone — someone who desperately needed him:

"Even though it's been two years, I still get this guilty feeling around Christmastime. I just can't help thinking about my brother Danny and wishing I'd returned even half the love he shared with me.

"Danny was born when I was four, and by the time I was six I had picked up on enough adult conversation to know that my parents were concerned about his development. He was, indeed, partially retarded; but my mother continually referred to him as 'special.' From the beginning this bothered me: wasn't I special in any way? I began to suspect that I'd be forgotten, except as a guardian for my 'special' brother. I decided to avoid that if at all possible.

"I still remember the day I cleverly slipped away from his clinging attention about a block away from our house. I tricked him and left him crying on the sidewalk so I could play with my own friends. When I started home, I found him right where I'd left him, beaming at me in spite of his tear-stained eyes and runny nose. Thankfully, he hugged my arm and murmured my name all the way up the block. I fully expected to be in all kinds of trouble for my foul deed, but Danny never said a word about it to our parents. In fact he came to my room that night to thank me for helping him when he was lost.

"You'd think I'd have learned from such an experience, but I didn't. I continued to tease him and to leave him out of my activities as much as possible. Any time Danny did show up where my friends were, I led the group in taunting him and calling him names.

"Through my high school years I avoided Danny almost entirely, having little to do with him even at home. It wasn't so much that I felt burdened to take care of him any more: I just hated to be connected with him because it might affect my image. I was relieved when my acceptance to college came because I knew that there I wouldn't have to worry about Danny's little feet clumsily pounding the pavement behind me.

"Mom occasionally wrote to me, telling of how Danny would sometimes cry for hours concerning his big brother's absence. She mentioned that the only consolation for Danny was that his big brother was coming home for Christmas in two weeks.

"Danny had been saving his money for over two years in order to buy a bike which he had seen some time ago in a store window. This would be the Christmas that he would be able to afford the purchase of it with his own savings. Danny was now thirteen and Mom had gotten him a paper route which enabled him to save a little money. He really was a hard worker and a real saver when it came to money.

"Though she didn't tell me about it at the time, Mom knew about Danny's Christmas plans for me. First she found his piggy bank empty on the floor in his bedroom; then she saw the shopping bag from Hampstead's Camera Shop. It wasn't hard to figure out that Danny had been listening on the extension when Mom had phoned me to ask what I'd like for Christmas. Danny had sacrificed his bicycle to buy me the camera I'd mentioned to Mom.

"At the end of the five-hour bus ride home, I was glad to be there. Walking from the bus station I looked at the Christmas decorations on the houses and thought only what a comfort it would be to spend ten days lying around my own house. Certainly I didn't expect what I found when I walked in.

"The front rooms were dark, but I could hear Mom's voice and I followed the sound to Danny's room. There, through the slightly open door, I saw my mother kneeling by Danny's bed, cradling him in her arms and rocking gently.

"Dad came up and took my arm, gently steering me into the living room where he explained Danny's accident. It seemed that Danny had seen a boy fall through the thin ice on Sluice Pond. Leaving the newspapers he was delivering, Danny ran to the boy's aid, only to crash through the ice himself. By the time someone fished him out, Danny was unconscious and remained so for several hours. He'd developed pneumonia and some other complications.

"Christmas eve came and Danny grew worse. That night Mom told me Danny wished to see me. When I approached his bedside, he immediately clenched my arm with his hands. Mom, on cue, entered the room with a wrapped package and handed it to me. I read the card attached: 'To my big brother who I love a lot. From Danny.'

"I opened the package and Danny smiled. Then he asked if I had a present for him. I really hadn't but I said that I did. I said it was so big that I had to leave it at the bus station and it would be delivered tomorrow.

"I hurried quickly out of the room with tears in my eyes and hopes of catching the store open where Danny's long awaited bicycle hung. What luck! The store was still open and I made the purchase. I carried the bike home and placed it in front of the tree, attaching a small card: 'To my little brother who I love a lot. From David.'

"All to no avail. Danny never saw his present from me. He never heard me say 'I love you.' He died that night in his sleep." (Adapted from Blaine M. Yorgason and Brenton G. Yorgason, *Others* [Salt Lake City: Bookcraft, Inc., 1978], pp. 36-38.)

Though the situation may not be as dramatic, there are those in the world who need you.

The gift at Christmas and at all times that the Lord asks of us is to feed his sheep. (John 21:15.) We are to love his children, even those who are apparently unlovable. We are to look beyond the surface into the soul. To offer the Lord gold and frankincense and myrrh is nothing compared to the gift of a loving heart.

ONE FAMILY

During World War II, the national pastime for all infantrymen was souvenir hunting. One day on a Pacific island, thinking I was perfectly safe, I strolled into a rather large cave looking for some memento to take to the folks back home. I moved about thirty feet into the opening and came face to face with an enemy soldier. We were both startled. The moment seemed eternal as we stood there staring into each other's faces. Then I thought he did a very gracious thing: he threw down his rifle and surrendered.

When I finally recovered my faculties, I took my rifle off my shoulder and motioned for him to move toward the entrance of the cave. In doing so, he stumbled and fell. It was then that I realized he had been wounded. As I turned him over, I discovered he had been shot twice in the abdomen and was in terrible pain. I bent over and immediately started to offer first aid. He mistook my intent and threw his arms over his face in an attempt to defend himself, thinking I would hurt him. Soon he learned I was trying to offer help, and he relaxed.

Several of our infantrymen were passing the opening of the cave, and I summoned them for help. In the process they brought in a Japanese-American interpreter, and it was during the interrogation that I learned a little bit about my newly found friend. He was a young man, seventeen years old, from Osaka, Japan. He had been drafted into the military at the age of thirteen and had been sent into China at the age of fourteen for two or three years of combat training before being sent to Okinawa as a garrison. I was nineteen years old at the time.

As we conversed, he wanted to know whether or not the American forces had bombed the city of Osaka, because that's where his parents were and he hadn't heard from them in a long time. He had a brother flying in the Japanese Air Command, and he wanted to know their fate at the hands of a cruel war.

He had big dreams for the future. He wanted to be a lawyer. He had a girl friend at home. All his words seemed so similar to my own, but the amazing thing was that we discovered we were both avid fans of the great American game of baseball — and, above all else, we even had the same idol. We both worshiped Lou Gehrig.

The more we talked, the more we found in common. We were brothers, born to be best friends, placed by some whim of chance on opposite sides of a bloody dividing line that was not of our making. As I finished dressing his wounds and placing him on a stretcher, he and I looked at one another and agreed that if World War II had been left up to us, we would have quickly shaken hands and hurried home.

Isn't it funny the things that we let divide us from one another, the superficial differences that are of no account in the eternal scheme of things? Too often we turn up our noses at those who are different from us and we build walls around our hearts, fortifying old prejudices. This person, we say, eats strange food; that person is a different color; he is too poor for my notice; she doesn't vote as I do and is therefore dim-witted, not quite bright; he lives in the wrong neighborhood. When we are looking for differences, we can find them in abundance. The fusses and feuds of mankind are usually much ado about nothing. I once saw a cartoon in which one ant snubbed another because he was too short.

When we step back from the problem of prejudice, when the given prejudice is not our own, it is easy to see how selfish, how blind, how damaging these walls between people are. Do you remember thinking as you read Shakespeare's *Romeo and Juliet,* "Why must some silly feud, some inconsequential nothing between their families, destroy the lives of those two young people?" But while we are clear-sighted at noting the prejudices of others, ours are so close to us that we wear them like skin.

When the issues of society are forcing us more and more into various pressure camps, when we are still divided by trivial external differences, let us train our eyes to see into the hearts of our fellow travelers here on earth. Our commonalities so far surpass any individual quirk we give them.

Carl Sandburg wrote these words in the prologue to *The Family of Man:* "The first cry of a newborn baby in Chicago or Zamboango, in Amsterdam or Rangoon, has the same pitch and key, each saying, 'I am! I have come through! I belong! I am a member of the Family. . . . Here are . . . landlords and the landless, the loved and the unloved, the lonely and abandoned, the brutal and the compassionate — one big family hugging close to the ball of Earth for its life and being. . . . Alike and ever alike we are on all continents in the need of love, food, clothing, work, speech, worship, sleep, games, dancing, fun. From tropics to arctics humanity lives with these needs so alike, so inexorably alike." (Edward Steichen, comp., *The Family of Man* [New York: Simon and Schuster, 1955], p. 2.)

And Montaigne said it this way: "Every man beareth the whole stamp of the human condition."

Life will bring to all of us experiences that are levelers — that will remind us of our common humanity, of our brotherhood, of our sisterhood — no matter what our apparent differences. Those who mourn, those who know the pain of labor and the exultation of childbirth, those who have talked to God all share a commonality that admits no distinctions according to race or ethnic background or political party.

I had a friend who was a landlord in an apartment complex. On one occasion he rented an apartment to a young Navajo couple that he later learned was financially strapped. Around Christmastime, the young wife asked him if he would extend the collection of the rent for an extra thirty or sixty days. He pondered her question for a moment and thought, "It's near Christmas. I can't afford that. I've got bills to pay. I have people on my payroll. Why would they ask me that question now?" But the spirit of brotherhood prevailed, and he agreed to wait to collect the rent.

That Christmas season the young couple with their two little children returned to the reservation to be with their families during the holidays. Upon their arrival there, they discovered their own family members were in dire need. An extensive drought had hit that part of Arizona. Of their 150 head of sheep, some 90 had already died. The family was desperate.

Back home, my friend learned of the situation, and without any prompting he rented a two-and-a-half-ton truck, loaded the truck with alfalfa and other needed supplies, and drove for ten hours to the reservation. With gladness in his heart and a joy I suppose men can't really measure, he unloaded the supplies for his far-off friends.

You can imagine the human scene that unfolded before him. Eyes of the women and children and even the proud braves were welled up with tears. The chief of the tribe approached him and, with moist eyes, repeated some words in Navajo that my friend could not understand. When he returned home, my friend shared the experience with an Indian friend who could understand the language.

"Did the chief say that to you?" the Indian asked in amazement.

My friend answered, "Why, yes."

And the Indian remarked, "Why, those are very sacred words that are reserved only for the greatest expression of gratitude. You indeed have been blessed."

It was another Indian who said, "With all beings and all things, we shall be relatives."

And that is the secret of it all. We are indeed relatives, "bone of my bones, and flesh of my flesh." (Genesis 2:23.) Belief in the brotherhood of man becomes consistent when we recognize there is one common father of us all. Once that truth illuminates the minds of men — that they are really offspring of eternal parentage — they can begin to see and appreciate their fellow beings as members of one eternal family.

Our Eternal Father in heaven is no respector of persons. Can we be any less?

I once returned to the battlefield of Okinawa. The devastated land was lush and green, and hardly a scar of World War II remained; but more importantly, the natives of that land are truly our brothers and sisters and, like my soldier friend in the cave so many years ago, we, too, shook hands and felt very much at home.

WHAT MARRIAGE PARTNERS OWE EACH OTHER

Black is the color of my true love's hair, Her lips are something wondrous fair. The purest eyes and the daintiest hands, I love the grass on which she stands," sang one young man about his lady love. She sounds like quite a woman, and the man seems to be in the very throes of high romance. How typical it is for those who have just fallen in love to be thus transformed, to believe they've found the perfect love, to settle back and get married, believing that — as in all good storybooks — they will live happily ever after.

But life continues after storybooks leave off, and spiraling divorce rates tell us that even the best romances, the most hopeful marriages, can end in disillusionment and heartache. Why? What is it that makes some marriages such a fertile ground for conflict? And, most importantly, if your marriage is one in which the relationship is strained, what can you do to reverse the trend and bring sweet harmony to your home?

Harry Emerson Fosdick said: "It is not marriage that fails, it is people that fail. All that marriage does is to show people up."

(Richard L. Evans, *An Open Road: Volume III of Thoughts for One Hundred Days* [Salt Lake City: Publishers Press, 1968], p. 28.) In that sentence lies the secret. Marriage shows people up for who they are and for what they are. There can be no pretending. In the everyday contact of life as we pass through heartache and disappointment and monotony and ecstasy, we see our marriage partner with all his or her strengths and weaknesses clearly exposed.

If any of us expect perfection in a marriage partner, we will be quickly disappointed, because perfection is too much to ask of anyone. We are all in various stages of growth, not yet fully realized. There will be days when our mate may disappoint us; there may be times when we see his or her judgment as fallible; there will be other moments when his or her failings seem glaring to us. It is then that we might remember the words of Richard L. Evans:

"But why should we suppose that we would find flawless performance in anyone else when we know that we ourselves are not all that others expect of us? Our judgment is not infallible. Our impulses are not always all they ought to be. All of us need understanding; all of us need explaining." (Evans, p. 65.)

Why do so many of us demand from our mate a standard of performance that we ourselves could never match?

We are, after all, living in an imperfect world full of imperfect people, and the happiest pair is the couple who realizes that there can be more joy, more happiness, and more love when there is more acceptance of one another.

Victor Hugo said: "The supreme happiness of life is the conviction that we are loved." (John Bartlett, comp., *Familiar Quotations* [Boston: Little, Brown and Company, 1937], p. 1067.)

When we consider marriage, we need to think not so much of what we expect from each other, but what we owe to each other. I remember one young teenage girl telling her mother that she hoped the man she married would be as brilliant as Einstein, as handsome as Robert Redford, as spiritual as an apostle, and as dynamic as a United States president. Her mother laughed and answered, "You can expect that kind of husband when you have become as brilliant as Madame Curie, as beautiful as Grace Kelly, as spiritual as Ruth, and as dynamic as a United States president."

The mother didn't mean to belittle her daughter: what she sought to teach her daughter is that all of us are in the process of becoming. If we discounted potential marriage partners for their faults, we would soon have no one left to marry. Just as we long for someone who loves us enough to understand our best intentions and our good heart behind our flaws and failings, so does our mate long for such a love from us. It is that kind of exalted understanding that makes a perfect marriage between two imperfect people.

A small item in a weekly newspaper noted the fiftieth wedding anniversary celebration of a couple. The reporter asked the secret behind so many years of wedded bliss, and they shared this idea: It seems that whenever the husband had a bad day at the office, he would put his hat on the left side of his head when he came home at night. If, on the other hand, the wife had had a bad day, she would put her apron on backwards. Well, it may sound a little silly, but it worked. Each learned to respect the other's danger signal, and each learned to read beyond the other's actions — perfect or imperfect — into the heart.

Perhaps this is why marriage is so demanding. We are called upon to give up all the selfishness we have as children that makes us as children look at the world strictly in terms of our own needs and our own wants. We are called upon to be mature enough not to see our mate just for what he or she can do for us. We have to learn that sometimes-painful lesson of considering our mate with wide, un-blinking eyes and loving in spite of all we see. We have to revel in the goodness and overlook the faults of those we love the best.

The famous German writer Goethe said: "The sum which two married people owe each other defies calculation. It is an infinite debt, which can only be discharged through all eternity." And, I add, it is a debt of understanding that creates in the giver a new heart.

That is why when marriages become strained, when critics assail marriage as stifling or old-fashioned or unworkable, I believe it is time to critique not our covenants or our partners, but ourselves. Are we not mature enough to take others as they are? Marriage counselors say that most couples come to them, spill out their troubles, and then ask, "Well, who is right?" Is your marriage still there? Are you pitting your will against your partner's in hopes you can remake him or her?

When you look for fault in your mate, there is fault to find. When you argue, hoping to prove some point, you both lose, because no one is a winner in marital conflict.

I am reminded of the story of Prince Otto Von Bismarck, the great

German statesman of the past century. "He once became so angry at the criticism of a professor that he challenged him to a duel. As challenger, he had to leave the choice of weapons to his opponent.

"When Bismarck's seconds presented themselves to learn the choice of weapons, they returned lugging a pair of sausages.

"The professor said in effect, 'One sausage is perfectly safe to eat. The other has been loaded with a deadly amount of trichina which will cause a slow and lingering death. If he will eat one, I will eat the other. He may have his choice of sausages.' "

"Bismarck was no fool. A man might die with some sort of honor on a duelling field, but never by eating a poisoned hot dog. He sent his answer: 'His highness has destroyed the sausages and asks that you be his guest at dinner this evening. After due consideration he feels he may have been slightly in error. He believes an agreement can be reached.' "

Whenever in our marriages we become duel-minded, whenever we pick faults, whenever we criticize and hope to remodel our partner, it may be time to remember Bismarck and the sausages. There is no honor in winning a marital battle. There is only loss and pain. As human beings there is only one climate in which we can grow and change and flourish: That climate is the one in which we feel the unqualified love of the one who knows us best. Let us each be capable of giving that kind of love to our marriages.

PART FOUR

THE DEPTH
OF CHARACTER

FORGIVENESS — THE GREAT HEALER

Paul Cezanne, the great French artist, was apparently also a very devoted father. One day he had just finished painting a street scene and a friend had come to admire it. As the two were conversing, they did not see Cezanne's five-year-old son approaching with a sharp toy in his hand. Suddenly the boy picked up his toy and repeatedly slashed at the canvas. Horrified, the friend expected Cezanne to explode into a rage, but to his surprise, Cezanne looked at the holes in his canvas quite calmly.

"Can you believe it!" he said. "My son has opened the windows in the houses." (E. E. Edgar, *Deseret News,* January 24, 1979.)

Most of us can't be that forgiving if someone destroys our evening newspaper, let alone an exquisite painting. But we find as we live through the traumas of daily existence that if we are going to survive without bitterness or frustration, there will be much to forgive. People are bound sometimes to rub us the wrong way; some will hurt our feelings, take unfair advantage of us, be thoughtless or ungrateful. How are we going to respond to these little unkindnesses? How are we going to respond to the serious hurt? Those who silently count up every wrongdoing of another find that their own burden grows heavier by the day.

You may have seen this kind of thing happen in marriage relationships, where each spouse quietly adds up the faults, the mistakes of the other. They may not mention it to one another, acting as if all is fine. But then in a fight, in the pitch of battle, the accusations come swarming out. You've heard it: "You did this; and last week you did that; and last month you did that." All the blunders of the past had not been forgotten and forgiven, but had instead been festering, just waiting for the right time to explode.

We often do the same thing when we relate to our children, tallying their errors, unconsciously waiting to let them know how miserable we think they really are.

But for our own sanity and happiness — let alone for the happiness of others — it is crucial that we learn to simply forgive those around us for their blunders and weaknesses. As one good Christian said when he heard someone loudly condemn another for some fault: "Ah! well, yes, it seems very bad to me, because that's not my way of sinning." (Clyde Francis Lytle, ed., *Leaves of Gold* [The Coslett Publishing Company], p. 73.)

And often, those things that seem so bad to us, so wholly unforgivable, only seem that way because they are not our way of sinning. Our way of sinning probably seems just as unforgivable to someone else. Are any of us so sure, after all, that we are not the ones in need of forgiveness?

As Joaquin Miller said:

> In men whom men condemn as ill
> I find so much of goodness still,
> In men whom men pronounce divine
> I find so much of sin and blot,
> I do not dare to draw a line
> Between the two, where God has not.

For the peace of our own soul, let us learn to forgive, to give others the assurance that in our eyes, at least, they are acceptable and worthy and ready to go on from here. In one of Victor Hugo's famous classics, he tells the story of Jean Valjean, arrested when merely a boy for stealing a loaf of bread to feed his mother's starving family. For this crime he was sent to the galleys for nineteen long years, years that corrupted him and made him one with thieves and rascals.

Upon his release, Jean Valjean was a despised man, an exconvict accepted by no one, until a bishop took pity on him. The bishop trusted him and gave him food and lodging. But Valjean repaid the bishop for his kindness by stealing his silverware and many priceless heirlooms. Valjean could not control his evil impulses.

Valjean was soon apprehended and was dragged back to the bishop's dwelling with the bishop's treasures still in his bag. The bishop took one look at Valjean, forgave him, and handed him his candlesticks as a gift. "My friend, before you go away, here are your candlesticks; take them," said the bishop. "Jean Valjean, my brother: you belong no longer to evil, but to good. . . . I withdraw [your soul] from dark thoughts and from the spirit of perdition, and I give it to God!"

Who can resist the upward pull of forgiveness? Valjean certainly couldn't. It was the beginning of a new life for Valjean, the dawning of virtues which had for nineteen years been sleeping in his tormented heart. He dedicated the rest of his life to charity and good deeds, himself befriending a lovely girl named Cosette. In the end he sacrificed his own life to the happiness and well-being of Cosette and her husband. On his deathbed, Jean Valjean spoke these words:

"I was writing just now to Cosette. She will find my letter. To her I bequeath the two candlesticks which are on the mantel. They are silver; but to me they are gold, they are diamonds. . . . I do not know whether he who gave them to me is satisfied with me in heaven. I have done what I could." (Victor Hugo, *Les Misérables* [New York: The Modern Library/Random House, Inc.], pp. 90, 1220.)

Each of us, being people and being imperfect, will have ample opportunity to forgive other imperfect people. Will we have strength enough to do it? Can we forgive the little hurts and stop stockpiling them against our family and friends? Can we forgive the grave offenses that call us to revenge? The great among us have done so. One family whose son was killed by a drunk driver learned that the driver himself had no parents. They took him in as their own son, giving him a second chance at life.

And Christ himself, bleeding and ridiculed and dying on the cross, looked out at his accusers and said, "Father, forgive them; for they know not what they do." (Luke 23:34.)

Our task — indeed our great opportunity — is to forgive those around us when they hurt us, for *they* often know not what they do. We cannot know how much they regret their unkindness, how hard they tried to resist it. We do not know the makeup of their hearts. What we do know is that our forgiveness may lighten their load and give them a new permission to be the person they want to be.

And when we forgive others, our own load will be lighter. Love will flood in where rancor used to be; joy will dissipate bitterness. Those who are forgiving find that this virtue is its own reward.

APPRECIATION: AN ACTIVE ART

Thanksgiving week is a time to roast turkeys, bake pies, and make our mental list of all the things for which we're thankful. And if we're common, our list may run in broad sweeps. We say our thanks in vast generalities. Sometimes we sound like the child who says a ten-second prayer: "Thanks for the turkey, my friends, my family, and all the other stuff."

But somehow in our wearied hearts, there is the inkling that there must be more to gratitude than these abbreviated thoughts, these large lumps that say, "Thank thee, Lord, for everything."

Sometimes we're a little like the twelve-year-old girl who was vacationing, traveling through the western Rockies by car: she spent every minute in the car reading comic books. When her mother asked her to look up and see the wondrous sights, she said, "Oh, if you've seen one mountain, you've seen them all." She hadn't learned the gentle art of appreciation. In actuality, it would take an entire lifetime to see just one mountain.

So what's wrong with our stony hearts when they don't swell with gratitude? Part of it may simply be our pace. The colors and shapes and textures of our life blur before us like a movie run too fast as we dash from scene to scene. Who has time to notice or care about small things like color distinctions? Purple is purple, not mauve or lavender or all the variations in between.

And newborn infants? "They all look alike," shouted one hurried man to two new mothers, as they cuddled to them their distinctively unique children, who felt sorry for all that he missed.

If you are wondering how anyone would have the time — let alone the inclination — to be so sensitive to small things, let me ask the more important question: How can we be grateful for the things we've never seen? How can we praise God for a world we've never noticed? How can we love and know our family and friends if we don't observe the silent, serving gesture?

The Lord made this world in extravagant variety with trillions of cells and trillions of stars. His work was careful, detailed, loving. He did not use just six plain colors or four basic personalities. He invested himself in each distinct effort. Why, then, do we succumb to the pressure to consume life like it were the fare at a fast food establishment?

The artist Andrew Wyeth said: "I love to study the many things that grow below cornstalks and bring them back into the studio to study the color. If one could only catch the true color of nature — the very thought of it drives me mad." Here was a man who was grateful for his world.

We can all learn to seek God by quickening our senses, our powers of observation. Some people may walk across an alpine meadow and call the flowers growing there common. But the botanist, the man or woman learned in the field, may rush from flower to flower with zest, pointing out to the unlearned the special medicinal powers of one, the struggle for survival of another.

While we are here amidst the plenty of this world, amidst the people who matter to us, let us learn to observe and praise. Do you remember what Emily says in Thornton Wilder's play *Our Town*? When she dies, she is allowed to go back and observe just one day of her life. She chooses her twelfth birthday, and it seems she can't say enough to a world that can no longer hear her:

"I can't look at everything hard enough," she says. "Wait! One more look. Good-by, Good-by, world. Good-by, Grover's Corners... Mama and Papa. Good-by to clocks ticking... and Mama's sunflowers. And food.... And new-ironed dresses and hot baths...

and sleeping and waking up. Oh, earth, you're too wonderful for anybody to realize you. Do any human beings ever realize life while they live it? — every, every minute?" (Thornton Wilder, *Our Town* [New York: Harper and Brothers, 1938], pp. 97, 100.)

Maybe that's what gratitude is all about. Most of us believe the Lord expects it of us as a gift or payment to him. But isn't a grateful heart really the greatest gift we can give ourselves? to realize life fully while we live it every minute? Perhaps that is why Cicero called gratitude the mother of all virtues — for it gives our days a keener edge, our lives a sweeter touch. Why let our time slip by unnoticed and unpraised until it is too late? Why take for granted the efforts of all the people who add to our lives?

How many hearts lie breaking because a life's effort was given without anyone's special notice? I remember reading the story of a woman who taught school for many years, and who, after retirement, received a letter of appreciation from one of her students. This is her reply:

"My dear Willie:

"I cannot tell you how much your note meant. I am in my eighties, living alone in a small room, cooking my own meals, lonely and like the last leaf that falls — lingering behind. You will be interested to know that I taught school for fifty years and yours was the first note of appreciation I ever received. It came on a blue, cold morning, and it cheered me as nothing else has for many years."

The art of appreciation — it all begins with noticing the wide, wonderful world around you and the people who make it even better. And that special looking demands that you call out a new power of perception, a new energy of hearing — that your very soul becomes as sensitive as the ears of a piano tuner.

If one person can make all the difference in the life of another by a word of gratitude, if one can thrill his own soul with an enhanced awareness of God's creation, the prayer each of us must say is, "Let me be the one."

"JUDGE NOT..."

Harold needed a raise. His daughter was getting braces on her teeth; taxes on his house had just increased; the family's Buick station wagon was about to roll to a dead and final stop; and inflation was making it tough even to buy groceries. There was no way for him to support all this without additional income.

"Ask the boss," his wife urged. "The worst he can do is say no."

Harold resolved to do so. All the way to work he muttered his speech to himself: "Mr. Thomas, I know my review isn't due for three months, but could you consider...?"

He could just hear Thomas saying he'd he glad to consider; but really, what did Harold expect?

"A little human understanding!" Harold muttered angrily in response. "A fellow can't predict these things. Goodness knows I didn't *ask* for orthodontist's bills!"

By the time he arrived on the job, Harold was really nervous. He made an appointment with the boss's secretary and went to his own desk, still muttering to himself. Thomas's door was shut all morning.

"Probably has a big meeting going on," thought Harold. "Probably asking everybody's opinion but mine. I've run my division efficiently all this time, but does he consult me? Does he even know how hard this job is? Or care?" Harold was really getting steamed. "Doesn't appreciate me, that's what it is. He'll never see that I deserve this raise. I'll go on sweating it out for peanuts until..."

"Harold?" Mr. Thomas's secretary interrupted his thoughts.

"Right," he answered. "Be right in." ("Jump and go at his very call," he thought to himself.)

Jittery and irritated, Harold stepped into the boss's office. "Mr. Thomas," he said, "I've come to ask... Oh, what's the use. I can't take it. I just can't live like this any more. I quit!"

That fellow who needed a raise is a little like all of us. We judge situations and people with very little information as a basis, and sometimes that judgment can lead us to wild, unfair conclusions. We call someone cold when he may in actuality be shy. We call someone incompetent when he may just be frightened. We call someone haughty when he may just be insecure.

A busy housewife drove her little economy car into the warehouse parking lot and parked it carefully. She didn't like being on this side of town — she'd heard about gangs of delinquent kids, and she'd seen the drunks in the doorways. Still, she wanted the best deal she could get on a washing machine, and this was where she had to come. Taking a deep breath, she hopped out of her car and ran quickly through the early dusk and the light rain toward the warehouse door.

When she came out again, the first thing she saw was a long pair of levied legs extended from the open door of her car. A young man was sitting in her seat, fiddling with something on the dashboard.

"Hot-wire my car, will you? You hoodlum!" she shouted, advancing angrily across the parking lot.

The startled boy leaped away from the auto, said something vague about light, and ran around the corner into the shadows.

The housewife climbed into the unharmed car and realized as she struggled to get it started that she'd left the headlights on when she parked it and had nearly run the battery dead.

The trouble with the snap judgments we make is that they lead us to diminish others who may, in fact, deserve our praise and love.

Most people are much better than we suppose. You do not know what burdens another carries, what secret grief weighs down his every day. When you meet a grouchy clerk, you cannot know what the customer said that she met just before you. Our Savior said it simply: "Judge not, that ye be not judged." (Matthew 7:1.)

Here is served a great truth. Of course, we cannot help but sometimes notice the faults of others, but do we not have faults ourselves? He who would live with only perfect people would live alone. And what a lonely existence that would be, existence on some imagined, self-fashioned pedestal.

The fact is that in the worst of us there are great gulfs of goodness, and to deny that by exercising a snap judgment is to deny something very basic and important. We cannot afford to deny goodness wherever it is.

Hugh B. Brown, a great leader and personal friend, told of an experience that happened to him in World War I when he was serving in France. There was in his regiment a man known to all of them as "unsentimental cuss." He was a man apparently without any feelings — a man not touched by things that affected most of the soldiers he served with, a man "who could stand by his comrades and see them shot down and never bat an eye." His language was coarse. He was given to debauchery and all kinds of crudeness, and the other soldiers looked at him and in their hearts became for the moment like the Pharisees of old who said, "I thank thee, God, that I'm not like that."

In France it was the duty of the officers to read the incoming and outgoing mail. One night when this man was on duty reading the mail, he came across a letter from a woman — Mrs. Jock Anderson — in Ontario, Canada. She had written to her husband and said, among other things:

"My darling, Jock. I'm so happy to have you where you are. We're all so proud of what you're doing. The ten little [children] are coming along all right. I had to wean the baby because I have to work to help with the separation allowance the government gives us. But we're all right, Jock, and if God should see fit to take your life, we'll carry on. But, oh Jock, darling, won't you plead with God with me that he will never allow us to receive word that you are missing? . . . Poor Mrs. Johnson next door received that word two months ago, and she's almost frantic. She'd much rather have heard he was dead. Pray God with me Jock, that I may never get word you are missing."

That was the letter this "unsentimental cuss" read. And that night Jock Anderson and five other men were called out into no-man's land on an extremely dangerous mission. Early the next morning three of them came back, and Jock Anderson was not one of them. Then this man, this unsentimental man, said, "Sergeant, do you know where Jock Anderson fell?"

"Yes, sir. He was on an elevated piece of land covered by a German machine gun."

"Would it be possible, Sergeant, for a man to go out and get his identification disc?" Each soldier wore a tag around his neck, and unless you could produce a soldier's identification disc or his body, you would not report him dead — no matter how many saw him fall. That rule was unimpeachable. And so the captain, this unlikeable fellow, said, "Could you get his disc from where he is?"

The sergeant answered, "No, sir, it would be absolute suicide, but if you say so, I'll try."

The captain stopped him quickly. "No, I didn't mean that. I just wanted to know."

That night the captain disappeared. No one knew where he had gone. The next morning a large military envelope arrived, and upon opening it the troops read: "Dear Major, I am enclosing here with the identification disc of Jock Anderson. Will you please send word to Mrs. Anderson that God heard her prayer? Her husband is not missing. He's dead." And then he added, as though it didn't amount to anything, "And me, I'm off to Blighty in the morning. The doctor says it's an amputation case and may prove fatal. Cheerio." Paraphrased from Stan and Sharon Miller, *Especially for Mormons,* vol. 3 [Provo, Utah: Kellirae Arts, 1976], pp. 169-70.)

That was the man who had the courage to crawl out at night alone in the midst of enemy fire to get a dog tag from a dead man's neck so his wife could have the poor satisfaction of learning that her husband was not missing. And many had said of him, "I thank thee, God, that I'm not like that."

Let us not judge others on our scanty information. Let us live by this creed: however a man may appear, there is something in him better than I.

JOY

Can you remember the last time in your life you really felt joy? When I say joy I don't mean that settled contentment that may be as usual in your life as the daily sunrise. I mean *joy*! I mean that stab of something so sweet that when you felt it, time stood still and life seemed bigger than itself. You remember — those high moments like the time you first fell in love, or the morning walk you once took when suddenly all of nature seemed in harmony with your soul and your sympathies seemed expanded to include the whole world. For most of us those stirrings of joy in our lives are just memories, and most of our time is spent merely surviving our pressures, trying desperately to avoid pain rather than trying to achieve that enlargement of the mind and heart and soul that is joy!

If you look carefully into your heart, you may find that there is something that you want — and want acutely — that life never seems to quite deliver. Do you know what I mean? No matter what you have, or what you become, you may still have longings that somehow seem unfulfilled. C. S. Lewis said it this way: "The longings which arise in us when we first fall in love, or first think of some foreign country, or first take up some subject that excites us, are longings which no marriage, no travel, no learning, can really satisfy." Lewis continued: "I am not now speaking of what would be ordinarily called unsuccessful marriages, or holidays, or learned careers. I am speaking of the best possible ones. There was something we grasped at, in that first moment of longing, which just fades away in the reality. . . . The wife may be a good wife, and the hotels and scenery may have been excellent, and chemistry may be a very interesting job: but something has evaded us." (C. S. Lewis, *Mere Christianity* [New York: The Macmillan Company, 1960], p. 105.)

C. S. Lewis suggested that there are two wrong ways of dealing with these undefined longings — these stirrings for joy — and one right one.

The first wrong way appeals to the world's fool. He is the one who blames the things themselves for not fulfilling his deepest longings. He spends his whole life thinking that if only he had married a different woman or had taken a more expensive vacation or had gained a more prestigious job he really could have caught the mysterious thing we all seek. You've read about him in the magazines. He is the one who jumps from marriage to marriage, from interest to interest, from country to country, each time swearing he has found the "real thing," and each time being disappointed.

The second approach to dealing with our unfulfilled longings is taken by the sensible man. He begins to see that nothing fulfills the yearning it promised, and he decides "the whole thing was moonshine." He believes that callow youth or the inexperienced may chase rainbows, but he knows better, and with grim determination he represses that longing for something more out of life. He calls himself a realist and sets out to teach himself to be satisfied with something less than joy.

The third approach to satisfying our hearts' longings — and the only right way — is the Christian way. As Lewis said: "Creatures are not born with desires unless satisfaction for those desires exists. A baby feels hunger: well, there is such a thing as food. A duckling wants to swim: well, there is such a thing as water. . . . If I find in myself a desire which no experience in this world can satisfy, the most probable explanation is that I was made for another world. If none of my earthly pleasures satisfy it, that does not prove that the universe is a fraud. . . . earthly pleasures were never meant to satisfy it, but only to arouse it, to suggest the real thing." (Lewis, p. 106.)

The pleasures we know here are only echoes of the joy that can be ours when we are reunited with the Lord and when we share his splendor and love. The sun's reflection in a dewdrop may be beautiful, but it is not as bright as the sun itself. The comparison is, of course, between something of infinite import and something very small.

The pleasures that we know on earth are not counterfeit; they are just not enough to satisfy our deepest yearnings. If we try to make earth the center of all our attention, we will spend all our time building false temples for ourselves, only to find that the good has flown. But if we aim for heaven, earth will be included as a bonus.

The more we approach the Lord with our lives the more we will see him in everything. And he, after all, is the author of joy for the whole universe, the very fount of joy. The highest joys here reflect the heavenly. That may explain why the very definition of gospel is *good news.*

Somewhere in the misty memories of my childhood in Arkansas, there is a Negro spiritual of great power; the words, vague now, still lift me:

> For I've got joy, joy, joy, joy
> Down in my heart . . .
> Down in my heart . . .
> Down in my heart . . .
> For I've got joy, joy, joy, joy
> Down in my heart to stay!

Closely followed by,

> I've got the love of Jesus, love of Jesus
> Down in my heart . . .

And continuing in the same pattern,

> I've got the peace that passes understanding
> Down in my heart . . .

And the final stanza repeats the first:

> For I've got joy, joy, joy, joy
> Down in my heart to stay.

The prophets testified in a similar vein when they said, "Adam fell that men might be; and men are, that they might have joy." (2 Nephi 2:25.)

Paul told the Philippians, "Rejoice in the Lord always; and again I say, Rejoice!" (Philippians 4:4.) There is in these three expressions no feeling of want, no sense of longings unfulfilled. In some unexplainable way, those who have focused on the Lord and his will, those who have recognized that all goodness and light springs from him, find every day more delicious.

Something will have to be done about the frowns we wear. If you have arrived at that dull point where you are merely trying to avoid discomfort and if you have given up all sense of joy, it's time for a change. You were meant to have more than that. I do not know who first equated holiness with austerity, but life in the gospel is fun. There are those who mistakenly believe that the religious life is a straitjacket, a series of shalts and shalt nots that bind our souls and bar our free expression. But a preoccupation with rules is only religion on its most elementary level. Those who have really discovered the Lord love him because, having seen the ultimate good, they can more easily see the good in everything.

A famous evangelist of my father's day, Billy Sunday, said that Christians ought to smile because they have so much to smile about. He was suspicious of those who have such long faces that they look as though they've eaten oatmeal out of a gas pipe.

Billy Sunday saw no conflict between joy and religion. In fact, he could not see how joy and religion could be separated. One of his unforgettable lines was, "God likes a little humor, as evidenced by the fact that he made the monkey, the parrot, and some of you people." Another: "Death-bed repentance is like burning the candle at both ends all of your life and then blowing the smoke in God's face." Whatever else, the Reverend Mr. Sunday was right about smiling. If the Lord dwells in our lives, we just have to smile.

Long ago, two boys were playing along the shore and the small docks of the broad Mississippi River, waving at passing riverboats. One of the boys said to the other, "You see that great big riverboat coming along? It's the Missouri Queen, and I'll bet I can get that boat to pull in here alongside this little levee."

"You can never do that," said the other boy. "If you could, it would be a miracle."

So as the great riverboat moved down the river, the lads waved at her, and when she came abreast of them, she suddenly swung in alongside the wharf so that they might climb aboard.

The boy who had doubted his friend was amazed. "How did you do that? Was it a miracle?"

The first lad responded: "It was no miracle. It was easy. You see, the captain is my father."

That is how it is with us, too. The Captain is your Father and my Father. He loves each one of us with a Father's love. And it is coming to know him that is the basis of our joy, our laughter, our smiles. When you long for something that you may not name, and when you grieve without knowing the cause, it is the eternal in you pulling for him and for his home.

HOW TO ORGANIZE
YOUR TIME

If I only had the time."

That's the best excuse around for not writing all those letters you've been owing, for not completing the odd job around the house, for not exercising and staying in shape, for not being all you were meant to be. In fact, we all say, "I can't do this or that because I don't have the time." We say it so much I think that we honestly believe that if we had thirty hours in a day instead of twenty-four we could all be perfect.

Michael Gore, a great American salesman, once said: "You won't find it in your wallet, or your bank account. You can't borrow it, you can't work hard and earn more of it. And certainly, you can't hoard it. In fact, all you can do with it is spend it." It's time, of course — the universal coin of achievement equally available to all.

Robert Ripley, the "believe-it-or-not" man, once pointed out: "A plain bar of iron is worth $4. The same bar of iron, when made into horseshoes is worth $10.50. If made into needles it is worth $355. If made into pen-knife blades, it is worth $3,285 and if turned into balance springs for watches, that identical bar of iron becomes worth $250,000."

The same is true of time. Some people can turn an hour into horseshoes; others can turn it into needles. A smaller number know how to change it into knife blades. But only a few of us have learned how to transform a golden hour into true-tempered watch springs.

Think for a moment of the person you most admire. Perhaps he or she is a high government official, a person with awesome responsibilities, one whose decisions affect millions. Perhaps he or she is the president of a giant corporation, the moving force behind a far-flung industrial empire, a person who must be up to date on a thousand crucial facts. Perhaps this person is a world-renowned scientist whose experiments have resulted in a better world for us all.

Whoever these people we admire are — regardless of their age, economic status, spirituality, or family background — they have not one second more of time at their disposal than you have.

They have merely learned how to spend their share of available time to the best advantage — to pack every working minute of their lives with meaningful, productive accomplishment.

If you knew what they know — how to eliminate the needless steps in every job, the proper way to start a day, what not to have around when working, the simplest way of reaching a decision, the easiest road to self-discipline — success in all your activities would virtually be assured.

Obviously, there are not many like these, for few people have mastered the art of getting things done efficiently. Most of us coast haphazardly through our days, relying on "inspiration," chance, and last-minute activity to do our jobs. We dissipate our time with the recklessness we would never permit in our handling of money matters.

How about you? Can you honestly say that you are using your time in the most fulfilling and profitable way? At day's end, can you look back with satisfaction to successful accomplishments? Do you regularly get the things done that you want and hope to do?

If your answer to these questions is a blanket yes, congratulations. You are well on your way to success. If, however, you find yourself shaking your head and admitting that your moments and hours and days could be improved, think about the following.

You would not dream of building a house before you had floor plans to work from. You would not hop into your car for a transcontinental trip without first consulting a map. Then why expect your use of time to take care of itself?

Behind every achievement, large and small, lies a plan. And if you really want to get things done, the sooner you learn how to plan, the better. It is really quite easy. All you have to do is this: 1. Set and define your goals; 2. Work out a definite program and timetable; and 3. Concentrate on essentials.

Let's take these steps one at a time.

First, set and define your goals. You will get wherever you are going faster if you know where you are going. Basic stuff? Perhaps. But most people bumble along ineffectually simply because they have never pinpointed precisely what they want out of life.

I remember a friend of mine who wanted to lose some weight. Rather than torturing himself by asking, "What's the use?" he found an old photograph of himself when he was slender, taped it to his refrigerator, and suddenly his willpower returned.

Make your goals for spending the valuable minutes of your life concrete and specific. If you don't know where you're going, your time just drifts by aimlessly.

Second, work out a definite program, a timetable. One day efficiency expert Ivy Lee was interviewing Charles Schwab, then the president of Bethlehem Steel. Lee outlined his organization service to Schwab and ended up by saying, "With our service, you will know how to manage better."

"Good heavens," said Schwab, "I'm not managing as well now as I know how to. We don't need more knowing, but more doing. If you can give us something to pep us up to do the things we already know that we should do, I will gladly listen to you and pay you anything within reason that you ask."

"Fine," answered Lee. "I can give you something in twenty minutes that will step up your doing at least 50 percent."

"Let's have it," said Schwab. "I've got just about that much time before I have to catch a train."

Lee then handed Schwab a blank sheet of note paper and said, "Write down the six most important tasks you have to do tomorrow and then number them in order of their importance. Put this paper in your pocket, and first thing tomorrow morning look at item one and start working on it until it is finished. Then tackle item two in the same way; then item three; and so on. Do this until quitting time. Don't be concerned if you only finish one or two. You will be working on the most important ones. The others can wait. If you can't finish them all by this method, you couldn't have finished them with any other method, either; and without some system such as this one, you'd probably not even have decided which one was the most important.

"Do this every morning. After you have convinced yourself of the value of this system, have your men try it. Try it as long as you wish, and send me a check for what you think it is worth."

In a few weeks, Schwab sent Lee a check for $25,000 with a letter saying the lesson was the most profitable he had ever learned. Over a period of five years, this plan was largely responsible for turning the unknown Bethlehem Steel Company into the biggest independent steel producer in the world. And it helped to make Charles Schwab the best-known steel man in the world, with a hundred million dollars in profit.

What worked for Charles Schwab can work for you. The logic is simple: you can only do one thing at a time. If you worry about all the other things you should be doing while you work at the one job at hand, you'll only drain your own capacities. Forget the other tasks awaiting you until you have finished the one you are working on. You will be amazed to see how much more profitably your time will be spent.

And, last of all, concentrate on essentials. We may use every minute in what seems to be a productive way, but if our minutes don't ultimately help us develop harmonious families, sensitive spirits, and peaceful hearts, then all our list-making and busyness has been for nothing.

What are you doing with your life? What are you doing with those precious moments that march by with unending relentlessness? As Thoreau said, "As if you could kill time without injuring eternity." (John Bartlett, comp., *Familiar Quotations* [Boston: Little, Brown and Company, 1937], p. 514.) The minutes of our lives are our dearest resource, more valuable than any hoard of cash or jewels. Don't squander them.

WHERE THERE'S LOVE

Some years ago, a number of famous men and women were on a talk show discussing the things that made them most afraid. "What do you really fear?" asked the commentator. And as these noteworthy people talked, they came to some areas of agreement. They were, they said, afraid of the power of the weapons man has at his disposal, weapons that could annihilate a population, decimate a city. They were afraid of energy shortages and crime in the cities. During most of this discussion, the usually talkative Bennett Cerf was very quiet, contributing nothing.

Finally, just as the show was about to end, the emcee turned to him and said, "Well, Mr. Cerf, you haven't said much. Isn't there anything you really fear?"

In a quiet voice Bennett Cerf answered, "There's only one thing I really fear — and that's not being loved."

When you really think about it, the motive for most of our actions is the great desire to be loved. We crave love like a plant craves water, and we do all sorts of ridiculous, crazy, noble, lovely things to earn the love of our fellowman. Those of us who sing, dance, write, play an instrument, or participate in sports do it partly for the love of the crowd and for the applause. Those of us who excel in school or on the job, those of us who buy fancy cars or diet until we're bone thin do it mostly just to earn the admiration and love of those who notice.

I know a young man who had such a strong need to be loved by a particular young lady that he sent her a letter special delivery every day for sixty days; and on the sixty-first day, she eloped with the mailman. Let's face it, being human means we have a strong need — an overwhelming, insatiable need to be loved.

I'm about to share with you the secret to the age-old mystery of how to be loved and adored by your fellowmen. This is it: *Stop working at it so hard!* Forget your desire to be loved. Concentrate instead on giving your love, your compassion, and your sympathy to somebody else. It's as inevitable as corn in August that when you do, the love will come flowing back to you in bushels.

An example of how this works is a story told by Arthur Gordon of a very successful business leader who gave personal encouragement and financial support for education to a young black man who worked for him. This help did not produce any immediate change in the young man's life; as a matter of fact, for a long time he failed again and again to put to any productive use the generous aid he was receiving. But the industrialist refused to give up on his employee; he kept giving him encouragement and, through his own faith in the youth, he slowly taught him to believe in himself and to succeed.

When this industrialist died, many important people came to the funeral service to pay their respects. But it was not the eloquent, smoothly delivered eulogies which moved them; rather, it was the love and the genuine sense of mourning evident in the manner of this young man as he haltingly and emotionally told them his story. With tears streaming down his face, he saluted his friend who had not only understood the importance of supporting success on appropriate occasions, but had also had the rare insight to have faith in a failure. (See Arthur Gordon, "The Healing Power of Compassion," *Reader's Digest,* April 1973, p. 185.)

Do you want to be beloved, lauded by all you know? I don't think the industrialist spoken of in the memorial service thought to himself, "I'm going to make this office boy love me" before he paid for the office boy's education. No, love was such an honest outpouring of his spirit, as witnessed in this single relationship in his life, that love was returned to him a thousand-fold.

Where does it come from — this capacity to give your love to others, to lift those around you with a single word, to share another's grief and feel another's pain? Let's look for a moment at the most famous of all compassion stories — the parable of the Good Samaritan. What could possibly have motivated this man to take a risk for a stranger — an enemy — by compassionately spending his time and money? What made this Samaritan different from the men who had previously passed this victim of robbers and left him on the road? Are we to assume that the Samaritan had nothing better to do, or that he was unaware that he was making himself vulnerable? I think not.

I believe the answers to these questions lie in the man's character and the practices of his life. Perhaps the Samaritan's first reaction was to feel sorry for that robbed and injured man; he imagined himself in such a predicament and sympathized. Certainly the Samaritan had courage: he was not afraid to get involved, to give, because it was right even though it might not be safe.

But I think the most enabling characteristic of the Samaritan was practice. He had the habit of helping.

I'm sure this was no isolated incident in the Samaritan's life. Through the years he had trained himself to respond, almost instinctively, to other people's needs. Loving and feeling with others is a delightful habit that takes practice just as does any major skill.

And people who are busy loving others don't have much time to brood on whether others love them. According to an old tale of the Orient, a Hindu merchant dreamed one night that he had died. To his bewilderment, he found himself standing in a large room, entirely bare of furnishings. Puzzled as to where he was, he looked around and discovered that there was a door in one wall; a small, neatly printed sign on the door read, "For the damned." Having no other place to go, he opened the door and entered.

In front of him was an enormous table spread with the rarest delicacies of food and drink. Seated around the table were a number of people; each was tied to a chair with his arm fastened behind his back. To the free hand of each person was fastened a spoon with a handle too long to be of use in getting food from the plate to his mouth. Although food fit for the gods lay within inches of them, the poor wretches were obviously suffering from the final stages of starvation.

The Hindu quickly backed out of the room and closed the door. It was only then that he saw another door bearing a sign, "For the saved."

He opened the second door and for a moment he thought he had mistakenly entered the same room. Before him was the table, spread with delicacies. The people seated about it were tied to their chairs with one hand tied behind their backs; a spoon too long for them to use was tied to their free hand.

Just before his dream ended, the Hindu merchant became aware of one great difference between the people in the two rooms. Instead of starving miserably, the people in the second room were happy and well-fed. Though their spoons were too long to use to feed themselves, they had realized they were not too long to feed their neighbors.

Each person in the second room was feasting, feeding on the greatest delicacies, while he fed his neighbor. What a true picture of love. Those who sat around that table and began to feed their neighbors did it in no calculated way. They hadn't thought, "If I feed them, then they'll feed me." No. Those who serve their neighbors feast on the greatest blessing — a life filled with love, both given and returned. A heart that gives always gathers.

So you want to be loved? Everybody does. We sing about it; we work for it; we seek it every day of our lives. But you know, degrees or fame or gold can't buy you love. Only loves begets love. Start giving of your respect, your concern, your sympathy, your praise, and your compassion to everyone you meet, because everybody else needs to be loved as much as you do.

Paul was profound when he wrote, "Though I speak with the tongues of men and of angels, and have not charity, I am become as sounding brass, or a tinkling cymbal.

"And though I have the gift of prophecy, and understand all mysteries, and all knowledge; and though I have all faith, so that I could remove mountains, and have not charity, I am nothing.

"And though I bestow all my goods to feed the poor, and though I give my body to be burned, and have not charity, it profiteth me nothing." (1 Corinthians 13:1-3.)

Be a somebody. With all your gifts, cultivate the best one — your ability to lift your fellowmen. And if you will, I promise peace of mind and joy untold.

DECEMBER'S MAD DASH

The last week in November is your last chance to take a deep breath before the busiest time of the year — the holiday season. You remember last year. December was almost too hurried to be fun. There were Christmas cards to mail; presents to be purchased for children and cousins and uncles and aunts; there were outside lights and tinsel to hang; there were parties to attend and food to prepare; and by the time it was all over, you were sick with exhaustion. Certainly you have heard the little poem which begins:

> See Mother. See Mother laugh. Mother is happy.
> Mother has many plans for Christmas.
> Mother is organized. Mother smiles all the time.
> Funny, funny Mother.

It goes on to recount Mother's list-making and her list-remaking, her shopping, cleaning, gift-wrapping, party-giving, tree-trimming, hurrying. And it ends with:

See the faraway look in Mother's eyes.
Mother has become disorganized.
Mother has become disoriented.
Funny, funny Mother.

Male or female, we could all use some tips on how to manage our time to survive December's mad dash. As one writer said, "Our days are like identical suitcases: all the same size, but some can pack into them twice as much as others."

Time management expert Edwin C. Bliss gives us ten ideas to make the most of our minutes.

First, he said, plan your days. Don't become so busy that you crowd out your planning time. The half hour you spend planning what you'll do with your other 23½ hours is the most valuable part of your day. Make a list and put your most important commitments first. Keep your list with you, and follow it.

The number two time-saver, says Bliss, is concentration. If you've made an effective plan for your day, don't distract yourself with worry. Don't think about what you have to do next. That kind of thinking just eats away at your powers and jangles your nerves. Give the project or problems at hand your all-out effort.

The next time-saver — take breaks. Fatigue cuts down your abilities. When the famous ad says, "You deserve a break today," it's right. You've heard the poem, "A Perfect Day."

Grandmother, on a winter's day,
Milked the cows and fed them hay,
Slopped the hogs, saddled the mule,
And got the children off to school;
Did a washing, mopped the floors,
Washed the windows, and did some chores;
Cooked a dish of home-dried fruit,
Pressed her husband's Sunday suit;
Swept the parlor, made the bed,
Baked a dozen loaves of bread,
Split some firewood, and lugged in
Enough to fill the kitchen bin;
Cleaned the lamps and put in oil;
Stewed some apples she thought would spoil,

> Churned the butter, baked a cake,
> Then exclaimed, "For heaven's sake,
> The calves have got out of the pen,"
> Went out and chased them in again,
> Gathered the eggs and locked the stable,
> Back to the house and set the table,
> Cooked a supper that was delicious
> And afterward washed up all the dishes;
> Fed the cat and sprinkled the clothes,
> Mended a basketful of hose,
> Then opened the organ and began to play,
> "When you come to the end of a perfect day."

Years ago, when I first heard that poem, I thought the only reason grandmother survived was because she took time off to sing at the end of her day. To be efficient, take breaks.

Number four — avoid clutter. Clean off your desk at the end of the day. Clean off your working space. Give yourself the psychological lift each morning of starting with a neat, well-organized environment. A cluttered environment makes for a cluttered mind.

The number five time-saving rule — don't be a perfectionist. Set for yourself a standard of excellence, but don't try for the unattainable. Don't be discontent with your best efforts.

Number six, don't be afraid to say no. If you are asked to add another commitment to your life that really isn't in the best interest of yourself or your family, say no. It's the only thing to do.

Number seven — don't procrastinate. Do the most difficult or unpleasant job first and get it finished so it will no longer plague your mind.

The eighth time-saving idea — delegate some of your work to others who may need or want some additional responsibility. If you have children, give them the chance to become involved in the holiday preparations. They'll love doing some of the jobs that to you may just be additional pressure.

Number nine — don't be a workaholic. More is not always better. During the holiday season, everything pushes us to do too much. Inspired by magazine layouts of the perfect Christmas, we make too much food, buy too many presents, and attend too many parties.

But the best time-saving idea is the last one. Do radical surgery on your time commitments, especially at this time of year. Analyze your plans for celebrating Christmas and cut out those things that don't really promote your happiness and harmony. Have you ever thought how ironic it is that we employ such pomp and ornamentation to celebrate the birth of Jesus Christ, he who chose to live a life of such simplicity and humble service? Could there have been a lowlier birth than his in a grotto of animals?

To remember him at Christmas, slow down. Take time to read the scriptures that record his life; gaze at the stars and remember how much you owe him; laugh with and love your family around the glow of a fire; serve someone who needs you.

One woman said: "I used to go home with my young family every Christmas to Mother's. I remember her running out to meet us with hugs; I remember her unhurried delight at small things. I don't recall at all whether the house was freshly scrubbed or the food done up with an ornate flair. But I went home because I felt Christmas there in Mother's love."

Decide, before it's too late, to slow down and let the holiday season be an especially enjoyable one for you and your family.

A CASE FOR CHASTITY

Toothpaste makers used to promise us that we'd wonder where the yellow went if we used their product. But these days white teeth don't seem to be enough. Toothpaste makers now promise us the ultimate for the young man or woman of this decade — sex appeal.

In fact, if you look on any advertising billboard, on any television tube, on any movie screen, you can't help but note that sex seems to be the uppermost thought of the day. Television producers have announced that program lineups feature many more shows with sexual innuendo all in the name of high Nielsen ratings. Madison Avenue advertising firms regard sex as the way to sell everything from cleanser to cars. And, of course, heroes like James Bond continue to dazzle audiences with their slick weapons and even deadlier attraction.

In an age when living together and unwed parenthood is as common as jeans at a rock rally, yesterday's standards seem to be vanishing away. I stand, however, with the humorist who noted that the new morality looks a lot like the old immorality, and adultery by any other name still hurts the same.

A recent study indicated that 40 percent of our young people will have had intimate relations before they complete their secondary education. Other evidence suggests that about 240,000 school-age girls give birth each year, which means that almost one out of every ten girls will give birth before she reaches the age of eighteen. Well over half of these girls are unmarried when they become mothers.

Because the strains of early childbearing are intense, those who become parents at a very young age are more likely than others to eventually abuse or neglect their children. Young mothers are also overrepresented in suicide data. Think of the toll in young lives that will never have their promise fulfilled, all because our society regards chastity as an old-fashioned virtue.

Counselors who work with young people report that many of them need and want support for saying no to sexual activity. In the face of a society that attempts to make promiscuity inviting, maybe adults need that same kind of support — the courage, the conviction to say no to any kind of improper activity outside the sacred covenants of marriage.

A frequently heard argument is that sexual indulgence is all right for "consenting adults." The relevant question here, though, is, "Why do the adults consent?" People frequently consent for the wrong reasons and foolishly do things that cause them regret and unhappiness for the rest of their lives.

The pressures are upon all of us to abandon our standards of morality. As we are bombarded with sensual, carnal stimuli that in years past embarrassed us, it becomes easy to first tolerate and then to accept practices that would have once offended our basic human feelings. Norman Cousins warned, "The danger is not that the exploitation of sex may create sex fiends, but that it may spawn eunuchs . . . people who insist on seeing everything and doing anything run the risk of feeling nothing. . . . Our highest responses are being blunted without our knowing it."

André Maurois's biography of the famous authoress, George Sand, describes her as a woman who was frustrated in her search for happiness in life. Like a moth beating against a lighted window, she went from affair to affair and never really found true love. (André Maurois, *Lélia: The Life of George Sand* [New York: Harper and Brothers Publishers, 1953].) Contrast her with the millions of men and women who have found supreme ecstasy and fulfillment in one home with one love bound in the covenants of marriage. George Sands discovered a hundred years ago what we must remember today — those who are willing to do anything will run the risk of feeling nothing.

There are many answers to those of you who are asking, "If a couple is really in love, what's wrong with their becoming totally involved?" Let's build a case for chastity.

First, the sexual experience is not a simple satisfaction of a physical need, like eating or drinking. It is the beautiful means our Father in heaven has given for us to provide bodies for spirits. As such, it is bound up intrinsically with our very identity. If used correctly, it can elevate and sanctify, make even sweeter the love of two who are committed and married to one another. If abused, it will violate and degrade.

Those who become physically intimate outside the covenants of marriage find their own self-esteem tarnished. They discover that they have taken the most sacred of physical acts and used it for their own selfish pleasure. Though they may not be willing to admit it, they have used the other person as an object, defining him or her in terms of bodily functions or in terms of their own selfish needs instead of by the other person's eternal value.

A second point in our case for chastity is that indulgence and experimentation prior to marriage may hinder a developing relationship. It takes time and work for a couple to come to understand one another. If, instead of building an eternal relationship with each other, a couple flees into sexual intimacy, they have not opened the doors to a deeper relationship. They have forever closed them.

Third, premarital intimacies create new problems that couples would never face were it not for their careless experimentation. Guilt is the big one. One writer said: "A person cannot always predict how he or she will feel afterwards, especially if one rationalizes feelings while progressing into physical intimacy. Yet, the next day, while facing himself in the mirror, he or she will probably sense that something in the area of self-respect has been lost and he or she will feel less comfortable about the relationship...."

Remember, God allows us to feel guilt for a purpose. You could rewrite all the laws and commandments, but you'd still feel guilt. The Lord, in order to protect us in our mortal sphere, built a special spirit of warning within us which we call our conscience. I remember as a young boy learning the little verse:

There's an odd little voice ever speaking within
That prompts us to duty and warns us from sin.

And what is most strange, it makes itself heard
Though it gives not a sound and says never a word.

A second area of potential discord is the doubts that can taint the relationship for both parties — doubts that can continue for years. Couples who have been unchaste think these kinds of thoughts: "Does he love me for what I am, or just for the pleasure he receives?" "If he loves me, why doesn't he respect my standards?" "Did she marry me because she loves me, or because she feels that no one else will have her?" "Is she comparing me with someone else?" Trust and faith in each other are lost, and no relationship can truly exist without trust and confidence in each other.

Fourth in the case for chastity is that it is not only possible but admirable for a person to develop self-control. Some people would have us believe that chastity is harder for them than for others. *Don't believe it.* The couple that has the self-control to wait until they are married to become physically intimate grow in respect and love for each other.

A television vignette showed a couple who decided to live together. The apartment manager said they could rent a flat for as long as they wanted it. Simultaneously she said, "We want it for five years," and he said, "We want it for a week." What a difference in commitment level! A piece of paper, a commitment to each other and to the Lord, does make a difference. Loving relationships are based on trust and on a sense of belonging. A relationship, even begun with ringing bells and flashing lights, will not continue to grow over an extended period of time unless a conscious decision is made to make it happen.

Fifth and most important is this: The best reason to be chaste is because the Lord told us to. He never gives us a commandment unless our following it will bring us peace, joy, and happiness in this life and in the one to come. A modern prophet reminds us that our Heavenly Father is not "an angry, cruel God who brings vengeance on people for not complying with his laws. . . . He organized a plan which was natural, a cause-and-effect program. It is inconceivable that God would desire to punish or to see his children in suffering. . . .

But however he tries, a man cannot escape the consequences of sin. They follow as the night follows the day. Sometimes the penalties are delayed in coming but they are as sure as life itself."

One who is unchaste will eventually pay the price.

Have you ever watched the surf pound in? It rolls and patterns the sand as it breaks upon the shore, but a few large rocks always stand firm. They are unique; they add character and beauty to the monotony of the sandy beach. They defy the fury of the breaking waves. Like the rocks, we must stand firm against the succession of ideas that pound against our standards of decency and morality. Everywhere we turn, we see people who follow the premise that chastity is out of date. But, if we stand alone, if we seem foolish and old-fashioned against the current mores of an immoral world, we must still treasure chastity. Our personal happiness depends on it.

PART FIVE

THE SCOPE
OF DISCIPLESHIP

CERTAINTY IN AN UNCERTAIN WORLD

In those happy days when the apple fell on Isaac Newton's head and gravity was discovered, people believed that there would come a time when science would be able to reveal all things. The secrets of nature would one by one unlock themselves; the world's geniuses would be able to give us an exact picture of the material world; the instruments of science would become so precise that we would have even a God's-eye view of subatomic particles. Oh, those were optimistic days.

But something happened along the way to fulfilling that happy, golden dream. We found out something about the nature of knowledge itself that was terribly disturbing. Let me tell you what I mean. Hold your hand a few feet from your eyes and study it. Certainly with the naked eye you can learn something about your hand's larger details, but if you wanted to isolate and analyze its finer features, you would need a microscope. There is something you ought to understand about microscopes. They can enlarge the image, but they cannot improve it; it is something like enlarging a small photo into a poster. The sharpness of detail is fixed by the wavelength of the light.

An enlargement of over two hundred times can show you an individual cell in the skin of your hand with ordinary white light. But to see more detail — to see a sharper, clearer image of that cell and the atoms that comprise it — takes light of a shorter wavelength, such as ultraviolet light, with a wavelength ten times shorter than more visible light. That sounds easy enough, doesn't it? If scientists want to get a clearer view of the atoms in the cells in the skin of your hand, all they need to do is to use ultraviolet light.

But that didn't work, either. In fact, even with the electron microscope, where the rays are so concentrated we can hardly call them waves, the picture of the parts of an atom is still soft and fuzzy.

Do you know what happens when we want to find out all about those billions of atoms that comprise your hand or the billions of stars that stretch out across space? We can't get a clear picture. The more precise our instruments with which to observe nature and unlock the secret of it all, the more confused we become, because the pictures are as imprecise and uncertain as ever. There do not seem to be wavelengths of light short enough to ever make the picture clear.

Centuries ago scientists may have believed they would one day know all things; today, they say they will never have exact knowledge of the world we live in.

Discouraging? Maybe it is. But the companion to this hopelessness of finding absolute knowledge in nature is even more discouraging. We live in a world where millions of people have rejected the idea that there exist absolute values of conduct upon which to base their lives and their hopes and their dreams. As Herman Hesse said, "A whole generation is caught... between two ages, between two modes of life and thus loses the feeling for itself, for the self-evident, for all morals, for being safe and innocent."

Many people have moved God from the center of the universe and his place has been filled with a terrible vacuum where selfishness rushes in. If there are no values upon which to base life, why not do as one pleases? What happens to our happiness when, as Earl Rovit warned, the phrase "Why not?" ceases to be a question and becomes an answer? Having standards and falling short of them is far different than having no standards at all.

T. S. Eliot called the generations of the twentieth century "hollow men," and Morris West, another writer, warned, "Without the Faith, one is free, and that is a pleasant feeling at first. There are no questions of conscience, no constraints. . . . It is only later the terror comes. One is free — but free is chaos, in an unexplained and unexplainable world. One is free in a desert from which there is no retreat, but inward toward the hollow core of oneself."

How empty a world without absolute values in it — a world that produces drugs, broken families, and students who never learn to read because they ignore all authority in school. It may sound wonderful at first thought — no "thou shalts" and "thou shalt nots" — but it's funny: a world without solid, unchanging values is making us miserable. Many of us have the sense of being fallen men and women. And I cannot help but ask, fallen from what? Fallen from a sense of the ideal that we carry with us in our secret soul from birth.

C. S. Lewis once wrote to a protesting, anchorless soul, "You say the materialist universe is 'ugly.' I wonder how you discovered that! If you are really a product of a materialistic universe, how is it you don't feel at home there? Do fish complain of the sea for being wet?"

What we all want, whether we've recognized it or not, is exposed in this little story:

A man watched a surveyor starting his work. He seemed to waste so much time looking around, tapping the earth here and there, that finally the man asked: "What are you waiting for? Why don't you get your instruments and get to work?"

The surveyor answered, "We must first find a fixed point — a place to begin."

Do you know what your fixed point is in this sphere? Have you found any certainty in this uncertain world?

Jesus Christ responded to each of his temptations with words we should remember: "Man shall not live by bread alone, but by every word that proceedeth out of the mouth of God." (Matthew 4:4.) Great scientists may not be able to find any certain knowledge; men, in fact, claim certain knowledge an impossibility, but that is because they do not have God's eye-view.

There *are* absolute standards upon which to base your conduct. There are secure values in this seemingly value-free world. If you have not yet found them, perhaps it is because in attempting to identify truth, none of us can always think objectively. For example, when a person looks at evidence with preconceived notions or conclusions already accepted as true, then that person is prone to see only what he wants to see and what he *needs* to see to support his preconceived conclusions. As a friend of mine said, "It is most difficult to judge the merits of two horses when your money is bet on one of them." Once you know where you want to go, you can often develop a magnificent array of logic and fact to support your argument. But this kind of wrongful thinking carries with it a high penalty, because reason doesn't give you the power to veto truth, especially revealed truth! You may reject truth — but you can't revoke it. Beware the trap of being absolute in your conviction that there are no absolute truths revealed by God in this world.

In Nathaniel Hawthorne's story, "The Great Stone Face," a man named Ernest looked in vain for his idea, whose likeness would be compared to the nobility of the great stone face on the mountain near his home. Finally, after many years Ernest himself was declared to be that likeness. (Nathaniel Hawthorne, "The Great Stone Face," in *Greatest Short Stories* [New York: P. F. Collier and Son, 1915], p. 120.) What was Hawthorne saying? Simply that he who lives long in the presence of an ideal at last becomes like it. And what of those who have no values, or whose values are as shiftless as the sands? I think we only need to look around to see the emptiness of their lives.

A modern prophet has said: "Back of the work, back of the sorrow . . . back of the life, ever grows the ideal. How constantly we keep our eyes upon it . . . determines whether we will fall as failures along life's highway or fulfill the divine purpose of our being."

There is one certainty in this uncertain world. It is timeless, unchanging. The Psalmist in the Bible sang of it thousands of years ago when he addressed this poem to the Lord:

"Whither shall I go from thy spirit? whither shall I flee from thy presence? . . . If I take the wings of the morning, and dwell in the uttermost parts of the sea; Even there shall thy hand lead me, and thy right hand shall hold me. If I say, Surely the darkness shall cover me; . . . Yea, the darkness hideth not from thee; . . . How precious also are thy thoughts unto me, O God! . . . If I should count them, they are more in number than the sand: when I awake, I am still with thee." (Psalm 139:7-18.)

DO YOU KNOW HIM?

During one of his missionary journeys, the apostle Paul visited the people of Athens and there found a disturbing sight. They had built a grand altar and were worshiping before it. Inscribed on this altar were the words: "To the Unknown God."

Sometimes I wonder how many of us who profess to be Christians are worshiping at a similar altar, worshiping a God we really do not know. Do we say we know Christ just because we have second- or third-hand information about him, information that may be distorted? Do we pay lip service to a Lord with whom we have no real communion? Do we call Christ Brother, but feel no real kinship?

Jesus Christ told us a single truth in many different ways during his earthly ministry. On one occasion the Master said, "And this is life eternal, that they might *know* thee the only true God, and Jesus Christ, whom thou hast sent." (John 17:3; emphasis added.)

When he was delivering the Sermon on the Mount he said of the day of judgment:

"And many will say unto me in that day, Lord, Lord, have we

not prophesied in thy name; and in thy name cast out devils; and in thy name done many wonderful works?

"And then will I say, Ye never knew me; depart from me." (Inspired Version, Matthew 7:32-33.)

We hear this same kind of message again at the end of Christ's ministry when he was relating the parable of the ten virgins. He told how the five foolish virgins pled for entry when they found the door shut against them: "But he answered and said, Verily I say unto you, Ye know me not."

Christ has told us, then, that entrance into the eternal realms of glory is contingent on our coming to know him. But the word *knowing* has many different meanings. It is one kind of knowing to read about a terrible automobile accident, and to feel pity for the injured and sorrowing; it is another kind of knowing to be at the scene of a car accident, to see vehicles twisted and demolished. But it is still a third kind of knowing to be in that car accident yourself, to see a car coming for you at a dizzying speed, to feel hollow and helpless as your car spins out of control. What a range there is in the knowledge we can have about a car accident.

The range of knowledge we can have of Christ is even broader. It's one thing to read about him, to learn something of his earthly travels and purposes. It's another thing to feel his spirit occasionally in your life as though he were an out-of-town visitor. But oh, what infinite joy there is in the kind of knowing of Christ where we can almost feel his hand touching ours, where his love makes of our secret life a holy land.

An ancient prophet said this of his coming to know Christ: "My God hath been my support; he hath led me through mine afflictions in the wilderness; and he hath preserved me upon the waters of the great deep.

"He hath filled me with his love. . . .

"He hath confounded mine enemies, unto the causing of them to quake before me.

"Behold, he hath heard my cry by day, and he hath given me knowledge by visions in the nighttime."

This prophet ended his song of praise with this plea: "Awake, my soul! No longer droop in sin. Rejoice, O my heart, and give place no more for the enemy of my soul." (2 Nephi 4:20-23, 28.)

Awake, my soul. Do you ever feel like that, like the best part of you is drowsing through your days? Awake, my soul. Do you feel a yearning for something that you can't quite describe? Awake, my soul. Do you ever feel incomplete, divided from yourself? We all feel that way — not whole because we are not one with Jesus Christ.

Life on earth for all of us is a short, hazardous journey. None of us escape pain. We may put all our efforts into a dream that turns to dust and rubble at our feet. Our bodies may ache and burn with sickness or age. Death may steal a loved one from us who was the very sunshine and security of our lives. Who, when all this happens, hears our lonely cry of anguish? When we kneel at the limits of our personal extremity, who has been there before us?

An old fable tells this story: at the end of time, billions of people were scattered on a great plain before God's throne. Some of the groups near the front talked heatedly, not with cringing shame, but with belligerence.

"How can God judge us? How can he know about suffering? He doesn't know what I've faced," snapped a joking brunette. She jerked back a sleeve to reveal a tattooed number from a Nazi concentration camp. "We endured terror, beatings, torture, death."

In another group a black man lowered his collar. "What about this?" he demanded, showing an ugly rope burn. "Lynched for no crime but being black. We have suffocated in slave ships, been wrenched from loved ones, toiled 'till only death gave release."

Far out across the plain were hundreds of such groups. Each had a complaint against God for the evil and suffering he permitted in his world. How lucky God was to live in heaven where all was sweetness and light, where there was no weeping, no fear, no hunger, no hatred. Indeed, what did God know about what man had been forced to endure in this world? "After all, God leads a pretty sheltered life," they said.

So each group sent out a leader, chosen because he had suffered the most. There was a Jew, a black, an untouchable from India, an illegitimate, a person from Hiroshima, and one from a Siberian slave camp. In the center of the plain they consulted with each other. At last they were ready to present their case. It was rather simple. Before God would be qualified to be their judge, he must endure what they had endured. Their decision was that God should be sentenced to live on earth — as a man!

"Let him be born a Jew."

"Let the legitimacy of his birth be doubted, so that none will know the identity of his father."

"Let him champion a cause so just, but so radical, that it brings down upon him the hate, condemnation, and eliminating efforts of every major tradition and established religious authority."

"Let him be betrayed by his dearest friends."

"Let him be indicted on false charges, tried before a prejudiced jury, and convicted by a cowardly judge."

"Let him see what it is to be terribly alone and completely abandoned by every living thing."

"Let him be tortured and let him die!" they said. "Let him die the most humiliating death — with common thieves."

As each leader announced his portion of the sentence, loud murmurs of approval went up from the great throng of people. When the last had finished pronouncing sentence, there was a long silence. No one moved. For suddenly all knew the Lord, through his son Jesus Christ, had already served his sentence.

That, of course, is just a fable, but there's a great truth found there. When Jesus Christ commanded us to know him, it was not for need of fawning admiration. It was because he knew we would, in our dark hours, need an unfailing friend we could call on, one who had faced it all himself.

Being the son of an earthly mother and divine father, he alone is in a unique position to help us. Having been mortal, the son of Mary, Jesus Christ understands the full range of our emotions and our struggles here. His sensitivities take in a broader sweep of both joy and pain than most of us can even begin to imagine.

But Jesus, the son of God the Eternal Father, is divine. He can lift us from those struggles, can change the condition of our being, the very soul of our existence. In the Garden of Gethsemane, he took upon himself all the cumulative weight of the sins of mankind with such pain that he bled at every pore and trembled and suffered in both body and spirit and prayed that he would not drink the bitter cup and shrink. He bore those sins so that, if we will but call on him, no darkness may ever grow so deep that it can swallow us. From that moment in the garden to this, it is his face that bears the stamp of infinite compassion. That is why he pleads for us to know him.

An old story tells of three men facing the final judgment. The first man went into a small room where he was greeted by a person dressed in white who asked, "Tell me what you know about Jesus Christ." The man told many incidents recorded in the New Testament about Christ's life; he had hundreds of scriptures memorized, and he even gave an archaeological summary of the lands where Christ lived. After this long speech, the person in white thanked the first man and sent him from the room.

The second man walked into the room and was asked the same question: "Tell me what you know about Jesus Christ." The second man said he had felt an occasional warm feeling in his life that he thought was probably the Spirit of Christ and that he certainly enjoyed Rembrandt's fine paintings on the life of Christ. The person in white listened carefully to this speech, thanked the man, and sent him from the room.

When the third man entered the room, he fell to his knees and, with weeping and great joy, exclaimed, "My Lord, my Savior; how long have I waited for this moment."

May I conclude by bearing my witness that I know God the Father really lives and that his son Jesus Christ is our Lord and Savior.

"COME FOLLOW ME"

I asked an extroverted friend of mine to try an experiment one day. I asked him to strike up a conversation with as many different kinds of people as he could and to request them to give him the names of one or two of their real heroes — those men and women whom they would like to emulate. Just ten of the many names mentioned by these people included: Florence Nightingale, George Washington, Abraham Lincoln, Pete Rose, Flash Gordon, David and Ruth, Albert Schweitzer, Albert Einstein, and Spider Man.

The list went on and on — from Babe Ruth to Roy Rogers, from Moses to Tarzan, from John the Baptist to the Hardy Boys. My friend reported that the experience was intriguing. Each person questioned was unique. Some were religious and some were not; some were well-educated and some were not; some obviously had money and some obviously did not. But they all had a hero or two — every one! I believe that's significant.

Just as a sailor watches the stars to plot his course, so do people need ideas, examples, someone whose life they can imitate. In the pressures of everyday existence, when the mechanics of just surviving confront us, it's too easy to forget our dreams — the character we want — unless its very embodiment is before us.

As a child I was taught, of course, to be honest. It sounded like an agreeable platitude. But I became converted to honesty when I heard that Abraham Lincoln had walked all those miles back to the country store to return a few pennies when he had been undercharged. As one writer said, "Example is the school of mankind, and they will learn at no other." No talking, no strenuous logic, no force or threat can change men's lives like the power of a good example.

It is said that on one of Captain Cook's exploratory voyages in the South Pacific, the sailors on his ship began to suffer from scurvy. Their tissues began to grow soft and bloody; their gums became brutally swollen; their teeth dropped out; and they became so weak that they collapsed on deck. Captain Cook believed that eating sauerkraut would relieve the sailor's plight, but he could not convince the men to eat it: the sauerkraut in its barrels emitted a foul stench; a rancid green scum had formed on the top of it. The men simply preferred scurvy to sauerkraut.

Then Captain Cook had an idea. In the evening at dinner the officers were each give one cup of sauerkraut — no more. The sailors were not allowed to have any. The officers were told that they could have seconds on other items on the dinner menu, but not the sauerkraut.

After a few nights of watching the officers eat sauerkraut, the sailors finally formed a committee to demand from Captain Cook their right to have sauerkraut for dinner, too.

You wonder if the power of example is that compelling? Let me ask you a series of questions. Allow yourself time after each one to think about your personal response.

1. Why are you dressed the way you are?
2. Why do you laugh at the things you do?
3. What has influenced the way you think?
4. What determines the way you act?
5. Whom do your children emulate?
6. Who are their heroes?
7. Whom do you emulate?
8. Who are your heroes?

These are complex questions, and their answers are all related. Almost everything about us is influenced by those we admire.

To a child, for example, the brightest star in the galaxy is his parent. Everything about the child's outlook is patterned after the example that his parent sets. Some friends of mine were telling me about an experience their little girl and her friend had one day. The mother was expecting another child and had been ill. She had not realized the profound effect her illness had had on the family until she heard her small daughter explaining to a friend, "Let's play Moms and Dads. You be the dad and yell about shaving, and I'll be the mom and throw up in the bathroom."

How many of us have such watchful eyes upon us — the eyes of our children, the eyes of neighbors or friends? And if these eyes are upon us, isn't each single action of ours, each single work, amplified in its importance? Like a pebble dropped into a still pond, how far beyond our movement does the circle of our influence spread?

Many people profess great desire to help solve the world's problems, to live their lives as a beneficiary to the human race. But as Sterling W. Sill said, "We have inspiring books. We have inspiring experiences. But the greatest of all good is an inspiring person." There is no gift you can give your associates or your children like that of a life well lived. There is no wonder as inspiring as that of a truly great human being.

When it appeared that the Nazis were about to overcome England, Winston Churchill fired his countrymen with new courage when he said, "We shall not flag nor fail. We shall go on to the end. We shall fight in France. We shall fight on the seas and the oceans. We shall fight with growing confidence and power in the air. We shall defend our island whatever the cost may be. . . . We shall never surrender." Was it Winston Churchill's words, or was it his jut-jawed determination that gave the Britons and the free world the will to win? One man's example. What kind of an example are you? Would you be proud to say to your family or friends, "Come follow me"?

There is one who has lived who was the perfect example. It was Jesus Christ who said, "Come follow me," as no other person ever could, for he knew that his way was *the* way for happiness in this life and in the eternities. His words speak to us across the centuries. But his life penetrates where even words are not enough. May we seek him. May we find him. May we obey him. And may we accept the challenge to so live that our children or parents or friends will have at least one living hero that they can follow.

TEACHING YOUR CHILDREN
OF A PERSONAL GOD

Have you ever heard the expression, "We did everything for that child, and look how he turned out"? Surely that must be the most regrettable sentiment parents can feel. But anyone who's been a parent knows that a child can pass through our lives, live with us every day for eighteen or twenty years, eat thousands of meals at our table, and still not absorb some of the values we hold most dear. You've seen it. The child of industrious parents may be lazy, shiftless. The child of a Rhodes scholar may flunk out of school. And most tragic of all — the child of parents who love the Lord may grow up without personal knowledge of who he really is. It seems incredible — but it's true. This can happen to even the best-meaning parents. We're all so caught up in the rush and hurry of providing for and feeding and picking up after the children that we don't realize some of the values they're failing to learn.

One mother said she didn't realize her three-year-old had little real feeling for the Lord until she noticed that her prayers every night were the same. They went, "Dear Lord, Thank thee for this nice day. Hope we have a nice day. Amen." It seems this little prayer got faster and faster every night until the words came tumbling out so fast that the child could not be understood. It was time, thought that young mother, to teach that child more about a personal God. But what about those parents who make a similar discovery in their teenagers when suddenly those teenagers stop praying or going to church? What would *you* do if suddenly *your* child walked in and announced he no longer believed in God? Sometimes understanding what's happening to our children comes almost too late.

All of us charged with the responsibility of rearing children, then, must stop our running long enough to took at them and learn what they feel. Do they know the Lord? Do they really talk to him? Has he touched their lives and changed them? Teaching your children of a personal God while it is still your precious opportunity is the most important thing you'll ever do.

Sandra Covey had a real experience with the Lord. She related: "As a child, the most profound experience I ever had with prayer was kneeling together with my father and older sister and brother, pleading for the life of 'little Linda,' one of our four-month-old twins.

"Overnight she had become ill — severely dehydrated and burning up with fever. Mother was at the hospital with the twins; Dad had come home after an all-night vigil and wearily gathered us together for prayer.

"We were all alarmed and a little insecure to see him so broken — so vulnerable — in the very depths of humility.

"I remember how [my father] begged and pleaded with the Lord for the life of that little baby, the tears streaming down his face. I also remember feeling that the heavens were opened — those pleadings were heard and received.

"When little Linda died," she said, "I knew the Lord had said no. I didn't understand why, but I knew somehow it would be all right." (Stephen R. and Sandra Covey, "Teaching Our Children to Pray," *Ensign,* January 1976, p. 59.)

How can we help our children have that kind of experience — when the very heavens are open? The first thing we must learn as parents is that merely telling our children about the Lord will never be enough. Teaching was never *mere telling,* especially when our topic is the Lord himself.

As Emerson said, "What you are shouts so loudly in my ears I cannot hear what you say." You cannot introduce your children to the Lord if you do not know him yourself. Words are not enough to convince your children of his love and constant care. They must see how much he means to you. They must see you pray and they must see you take your troubles to him. They must sense that you rely on him.

When one father was asked how he reared such a fine family, he simple answered, "On my knees." Don't you think that family caught his spirit, his delight in the Lord almost in the very air they breathed at that home?

I once had a little three-year-old sitting on my lap who sang a wonderful Primary song about being a child of God. When she finished I said, "You sing as though you know God." She nodded, "Yes!" I asked, "How would a three-year-old know God?" She replied, "Because I have a father."

Psychologists tell us that a child's first concept of God is often based on his attitude toward his own parents. If that relationship is distorted, the child may grow up with a distorted view of the Lord, which may color that relationship for the child forever. If, for example, a parent is unkind or overly critical, the child might see the Lord that way. His prayers will become cover-ups to hide his problems from the Lord, who he believes sees him as critically as his parents do. We could find lots of other examples, but the point is this: Our children will see the Lord as they see us, until personal revelation from him expands their point of view. What a heavy responsibility that gives parents to teach by example, to love unconditionally, to forgive imperfections.

So, in teaching our children about a personal God, real example is the first principle; the second principle is similar: we must give our children personal experience with prayer. Many of us think we have done our duty if we teach our children to "say" their prayers. And that is a worthwhile discipline. Surely children must learn from their parents the helpful habit of a nightly prayer and a regular prayer over the food. But that is not enough, because a mechanical prayer may not reach the Lord, and that is our ultimate aim — communication with him, letting his presence fill and flood our lives.

Our goal, then, is to teach our children to talk to their Heavenly Father about their real feelings, to make their prayers heartfelt. One family accomplishes this at family prayer by pausing a few moments before they rush into it, recognizing that family members have come from distracting activities all over the house and are not focusing on heavenly things. They sing a favorite hymn or read a scripture; they just ponder to whom they are about to speak. But it helps each family member assume a prayerful attitude. Next they ask each family member if he needs special help with anything, what requests he has of the Lord. They speak of the happiest moments of the day, the ways in which they've been blessed. Then they are ready for prayer — and it's "a different," more sincere prayer than it would have been just five minutes earlier. This process can work as well with a single child as it does with an entire family. And it's the best five minutes you'll spend in the day.

Last, teach your children to listen to the Lord. Teach them what kinds of answers they can expect from him. The scriptures refer to it as "learning to ponder." Help your children sense when the Lord is helping them in their lives. There are so many loud voices in this world, they may not hear the still small one unless you teach them how it sounds.

As parents, we cannot forfeit our children to a life without the Lord because we neglected to introduce them. We who know the Lord, who have felt the heavens open and receive our prayers, understand that that dear friendship is the most priceless gift we can give our children.

In modern scripture there is a story about some young warriors who fought valiantly, unafraid of death, to preserve their liberty and homes. Why were they so brave? We are told that "they had been taught by their mothers, that if they did not doubt, God would deliver them." And as they rehearsed the words of their mothers concerning the love of the Lord for them they said, "We do not doubt our mothers knew it." (Alma 56:47-48.)

Let us teach our children, that they will not doubt, and that they may learn to love the Lord.

I'LL BE HOME
FOR CHRISTMAS

Once during an era many have forgotten, we had a Christmas song. It came to us in a war-torn world while we were stationed what seemed like a million miles west of Pearl Harbor, and we sang it with tears in our eyes because we were pretty sure it would not come true.

"I'll be home for Christmas. You can count on me. Please have snow and mistletoe and presents 'round the tree. Christmas Eve will find me where the love-light gleams. I'll be home for Christmas if only in my dreams." And because it was wartime for many who sang that song, it was the last Christmas they had on this earth.

We would all like to be home for Christmas during that special season "where the love-light gleams." Stored in our memories are pleasant moments, warm moments that have touched our hearts and stayed with us forever — the piney smell of the Christmas tree, the broken ornaments that had to be situated on the mantel year after year, the sweet aroma of Christmas cookies baking in the oven, the love in the eyes of dear ones. We remember these times as some of the sweetest in life.

But have you noticed lately that sometimes Christmas isn't quite what you thought it would be? No smell is as pungent, no moment as dear as those you seem to remember. Do you ever feel you have lost something along the way? Do you ever yearn for something and not know what it is?

A small child woke up from a dream and told her father: "I dreamed I was lost and I was scared. I went all over the city looking for my home, but I couldn't find it anywhere. I looked at homes of different shapes and sizes, but none of them was mine. I asked everyone I saw, but no one knew where to find my home."

"I'll be home for Christmas." It is a yearning sort of song. Christmastime itself is a yearning sort of season, and, like this child who dreamed she was lost, we search everywhere to find that sweet something that makes our lives complete — and all the tinsel and presents and sweets will never do it.

The sweet something we long for in our lives can only come from one source — our Heavenly Father and his son, Jesus Christ, whose very birth we celebrate at Christmas. And if we ever banish ourselves from them through indifference, disbelief, or just the daily duties that drive us away from the truly important things, we will never find what we really want in life.

Of course, many believe they have wonderful reasons to forget Jesus Christ at Christmas and during all other times of life. "I am too busy," says one group. "Who has time for things like that?" "I just can't pray" says someone else. "It doesn't work for me." "I am out for myself," says another, and then he wonders why happiness eludes him.

It reminds me of the Christmas story told by one of the innkeepers who couldn't find room for Joseph and Mary: "What could be done? The inn was full of folk. . . .

"That they were so important — just the two — no servants, just a workman sort of man, leading a donkey, and his wife thereon, drooping and pale. I saw them not myself. My servants must have driven them away. But had I seen them, how was I to know?

"Were inns to welcome stragglers, up and down in all our towns from Beersheba to Dan, till He should come? And how were men to know? There was a sign, they say, a heavenly light resplendent; but I had no time for stars. And there were songs of angels in the air out on the hills. But how was I to hear amid the thousand clamors of an inn?'' (Amos R. Wells, ''The Bethlehem Inn Keeper,'' comp. George Bickerstaff, *Christmas Readings for the L.D.S. Family* [Salt Lake City: Bookcraft, Inc., 1967], p.1.)

Christmastime presents a thousand clamors in our lives. Every day of life leaves us as was the innkeeper, saying, ''no time for stars or angels' songs.'' But how foolish this innkeeper seems when he says, ''How was I to know?'' How foolish each of us will appear if we cut ourselves off from the Lord, and then, after missing it all our lives, we can only say, ''But how was I to know?''

Make Christmastime not just a time to receive the socks, ties, bathrobe, and perfume all glittery and wrapped under your tree. Receive at Christmas the ultimate gift.

''For God so loved the world, that he gave his only begotten Son, that whosoever believeth in him should not perish, but have everlasting life.'' (John 3:16.)

And the wonder of God's gift to man, his only begotten Son — is not just that this son was called ''Wonderful, Counsellor, The mighty God, The everlasting Father, The Prince of Peace'' (Isaiah 9:6) — the wonder is that he was born among us as a little child, that his mother carried him and nursed him with loving trust, that he was divine yet subjected himself to work with common man, that he grew line upon line, that he suffered pain and sorrow, that his feet grew dusty as he walked the roads of Galilee.

Divine, oh yes; but since he came as a child and worked with us, his life introduces to our every day the purpose of the sameness in our souls and destinies. He understands our feelings, our needs, our ultimate longings as no one else can.

There is an old story about the wise men — two were old and stern and one was young. As they mounted their camels with their sacks of treasure for Christ, the youngest one stopped them and went in a high chamber to which he had not been since he was a child. He rummaged around and eventually came back out and approached the caravan. In his hand he carried something that glittered in the sun.

The two old kings thought the young king had brought some new gift more rare and precious than any they had been able to find in all their treasure rooms, but suddenly the young king took out of his hand a dog made of tin, painted white and speckled with black spots where the paint was worn away. The toy shone in the sun as if it had been silver.

The young wise man turned a key in the side of the little black and white dog, and when the king stepped aside, the dog leaped high into the air and turned a somersault. It turned another and another and then rolled over on its side and lay there with its paint showing.

A child, the son of a camel driver, laughed and clapped his hands. He smiled with delight. The kings, however, were stern.

"What folly has seized you?" growled the eldest of the wise men. "Is this a gift to bring to the king of kings?"

And the young man answered and said, "For the king of kings there are true gifts of great worth — gold, frankincense, and myrrh. But this," he said, "is for the child of Bethlehem."

Jesus Christ came to us, after all, as a little child — and though he wore the mantle of divinity, he knew the frailties, the longings in each of us. And when we have a yearning and we don't know what it is for, it could be our soul longing for its heartland, longing to be no longer cut off from the Lord.

"I'll be home for Christmas. You can count on me." Rather than filling the Christmas season with memories of simple trinkets and carols, let us fill up our souls with the unspeakable joy of knowing that God lives and loves us.

THE POWER OF PRAYER

 M any people in this world have stopped praying. Or if they do pray, their prayers are perfunctory, a duty to quickly dispense with. Are you one of those, one of the lonely people on this earth who haven't yet met God? Are you wandering through your days without direction, solace, fulfillment?

I've heard all the excuses. There are those who say that God is dead and removed to some far corner of the universe; others claim that the Lord is only the product of wishful thinking by those who cannot deal with life's harsh realities. Then there are those who acknowledge his existence, but who feel they are just too busy to make the acquaintance.

Well, we may ignore the Lord; we may abandon him on the flimsiest pretense, but for every soul who walks this earth there will come a time when experience or tragedy or disappointment will plunge him to the very depths of his own existence. If at that time he cannot call with confidence upon a Higher Power, there will be no comfort. There can be no loneliness like that of being cut off from our very Maker.

Ponder these words from Charles Gounod's song, "O Divine Redeemer": "Ah, Turn me not away; receive me though unworthy, Hear thou my cry, behold, Lord my distress. Answer me from Thy throne . . . O regard me." Think about those words. "O regard me." Isn't that the deepest wish in each of our hearts, to be regarded? to have someone completely understand our yearnings and troubles? to have comfort when there is no comfort to be found? Yet, that is only part of the promise the Lord holds out to those who will seek him. There are needs in the human heart that can be met by no one but the Lord.

Do you remember the event in Christ's life when many of his followers left and would walk no more with him?

"Then said Jesus unto the twelve, Will ye also go away?

"Then Simon Peter answered him, Lord, to whom shall we go? thou hast the words of eternal life." (John 6:67-68.)

Those are poignant words: "Lord, to whom shall we go?" for, of course, there is only one answer. For guidance down the wandering mortal path, for peace when the waters are stormy, the only person to whom we can turn is the Lord. And we must not come to him as strangers.

If you have not prayed to the Lord, if your prayers are merely thoughtless repetitions, today is the day to begin to know him, to learn to pray with real intent, expecting to be heard.

Think back to the scene in the Garden of Gethsemane when Jesus poured out his soul to his Father with pleadings such as have never been equaled. Here was a prayer of petition, of glory and adoration. Especially note this verse from the account: "And being in an agony he prayed more earnestly: and his sweat was as it were great drops of blood falling down to the ground." (Luke 22:44.) Bruce McConkie says of this passage: "Now here is a marvelous thing. Note it well. The Son of God 'prayed more earnestly'! He who did all things well, whose every word was right, whose every emphasis was proper; he to whom the Father gave his Spirit without measure; he who was the only perfect being ever to walk the dusty paths of planet earth — the Son of God 'prayed more earnestly. . . .' " (Bruce R. McConkie, "Why the Lord Ordained Prayer," *Ensign*, January 1976, p. 8.)

As I ponder this verse, I cannot help but wonder if each of us might not pray more earnestly, with more preparation, more thought, more desire. Do we *hunger* and *thirst* after the Lord, or are we so glutted with earthly sensation and duty that we forsake our sweetest opportunity? A modern prophet said, "There are too many of us content to dwell in the slums of the intellect and of the spirit. Too many of us seek for happiness in the sunless surrounding of indulgence." (Clare Middlemiss, comp., *Man May Know for Himself: Teachings of President David O. McKay* [Salt Lake City: Deseret Book Company, 1969], p. 186.) Oh, what a sorrow to pass through life and miss the Lord simply because we were lazy.

When you pray and do not feel his presence, it is not because he has moved. He has not taken time off — but maybe you have. Must it take a crisis to bring you back to your knees?

The Lord wants to answer your prayers. I remember reading of a young bride who was terribly frightened because her husband had left town on a business trip. She had not stayed alone since she was a child, having been the victim of an attempted attack — at night, when she had been alone. This night alone, with her husband gone, she was terribly frightened. The normal groans and creaks from her old house evoked visions of prowlers. She shut off her television set, turned on several lights, and paced nervously from one room to another. Finally, she realized that she couldn't face the next twenty-four hours in that frame of mind, so, summoning up all her courage, she turned off the lights and went into the bedroom.

She sat on the bed and tried to get control of her fears, but in desperation she cried out to the Lord to comfort her and bring peace to her frightened soul. Just as she finished her plea, she seemed to hear in her mind the strains of a simple melody, coming unbidden and at first unnoticed. But as the music continued, it captured her entire attention. It was a Church hymn, but it wasn't a familiar hymn and she couldn't remember the title or the words.

She relaxed and listened intently as the hymn rang on through her heart until it broke into the final glorious stanza. At that point the words of the song came into her mind with perfect clarity and conviction: "My noonday walks he will attend, And all my silent midnight hours defend." ("The Lord My Pasture Will Prepare," *Hymns*, no. 113.) With this, she said, her soul was filled from the center outward with such a wave of sweet warmth that she rested well that night, knowing the Lord gave her comfort and peace. (Melva Lee Wheelwright, "My First Night Alone," *Ensign*, January 1976, p. 48.)

Examples like this one abound, and the Lord has blessed and aided his children through both the dramatic and daily events of life. He wants to bless you and me. But to be sensitive to his guidance and solace we must every day become more spiritually receptive, become — step by step — sensitive to his touch. We must become mighty listeners. These are not necessarily abilities with which we are born. They are talents accrued through daily prayer. It is only through prayer that we learn the how and when and what of prayer.

And is the effort worth it? I am with Mary Gardiner Brainard when she said, "I would rather walk with God in the dark than go alone in the light." (Richard L. Evans, *Richard Evans' Quote Book* [Salt Lake City: Publishers Press, 1971], p. 127.)

THE LIGHT
OF CHRISTMAS

At the Christmas season we string up lights against dark streets and celebrate the birth of Jesus Christ. But even before Christ was born, the inhabitants of the earth observed this season as a special time. Long before precise calendars and clocks, all that people who lived in northern Europe could tell was that in this season the days grew shorter and shorter, the night ever longer and darker, as if the sun itself was dying.

Can you be there in imagination with those men and women who depended upon the sun as a source of life, of fertility? Can you imagine the fear they must have felt as the earth itself froze, food became scarce, and the sun seemed to dwindle? The Druids sent out runners to the tops of the hills to watch for that moment when the sun had reached its lowest point in the heavens and was ready to return. In Scandinavian countries great fires were kindled to defy the Frost King. These early peoples gathered around fires to comfort one another and to look forward to the breaking of the ice when their ships might again embark.

To these northern people, the sun was considered a wheel that alternately threw its glow upon the earth and away from it — and oh, the rejoicing at the winter cycle when the sun began to rise over the world with renewed vigor and power after having sunk to its low point in the heavens. We get our word *yule* from this ancient idea of a sun wheel.

I've often thought that though we may have little in common with these ancient, superstitious people, our celebration of Christmas is still a celebration of light's triumph over darkness.

Our Heavenly Father himself chose to mark the birth of his son with a new light in the universe. We read in Matthew, "Now when Jesus was born in Bethlehem of Judaea in the days of Herod the king, behold, there came wise men from the east to Jerusalem, Saying, Where is he that is born King of the Jews? for we have seen his star in the east, and are come to worship him." (Matthew 2:1-2.) Tradition has it that these wise men and their fathers and grandfathers before them had watched for the star that meant the Christ was born.

Do you have need in your life for a light, a steady beacon that charts the way through this dark wilderness that is mortality? Most of us do. We need to know that even when life fragments us and beats us and throws us against personal hazard that we are loved. We *yearn* for that love and understanding. We need to know that the most powerful being in the universe knows us by name. It was Paul who said, "For I am persuaded, that neither death, nor life, nor angels, nor principalities, nor powers, nor things present, nor things to come, Nor height, nor depth, nor any other creature, shall be able to separate us from the love of God, which is in Christ Jesus our Lord." (Romans 8:38-39.)

Having been mortal, Christ, as no one else, understands the full range of our emotions, our struggles here. His sensitivities took in a broader sweep of both joy and pain than we can imagine — all that he might succor his people. When you kneel at the very limits of your personal extremity, he has been there before you.

Think of his birth. It is a story of poverty. Luke tells us that Mary and Joseph sought refuge for the night, but that there was no room for them in the inn. I wonder, had they been richer or more influential, or perhaps had they known the right people, if a room couldn't have been found for them. Mary, after all, was probably suffering the first pangs of labor — or at least she was in great misery, having ridden a long distance on a donkey just as she was ready to deliver.

But no room was found. Not for this birth. How must Mary and Joseph have felt retreating to a stable full of animals to bear God's own child? In thinking of this, Jeffrey R. Holland, a great educator, said: "I was a student . . . just finishing my first year of graduate work when our first child, a son, was born. We were very poor, though not so poor as Joseph and Mary. My wife and I were both going to school, both holding jobs. . . . We drove a little Volkswagen which had a half-dead battery because we couldn't afford a new one (Volkswagen *or* battery).

"Nevertheless, when I realized that our own night of nights was coming, I believe I would have done any honorable thing in this world, and mortgaged any future I had, to make sure my wife had the clean sheets, the sterile utensils, the attentive nurses, and the skilled doctors who brought forth our firstborn son. If she or that child had needed special care at the Mayo Clinic, I believe I would have ransomed my very life to get it." (Jeffrey R. Holland, "Maybe Christmas Doesn't Come From a Store," *Ensign*, December 1977, pp. 64-65.)

Did Joseph feel any different? What was the sting in his heart as he cleared away the dirty straw — the stable litter — and prepared a place for Mary to deliver God's own son? Could there be a worse, more disease-ridden spot for a child to be born? Surely for this birth there ought to be scores of attendants to soothe the mother, to mop her troubled brow. Surely there should be a doctor to help this Mary, herself hardly more than a child. But none of this was to be. Alone and unattended, without fanfare or mortal notice, Mary brought forth Jesus Christ, the Light of the world. There was no sweet linen to wrap the baby in and there was no comfort for the exhausted mother, but this was the central point of all human history, and the beginning of a life that was to descend below all things. Why? So that having experienced pain, humiliation, temptation, loneliness, and disappointment, Jesus Christ could be the Light at the end of your and my dark tunnel.

Today there are many who dispute that Jesus Christ was sent from his Father to be a Light unto the world, the only Light. The so-called philosophical voices among us proclaim him to be instead a great teacher, the son of Mary and Joseph, the greatest moralist of all time, a product of our need to believe, as great as Mohammad, a significant influence on the world. The list goes on and on. But I bear my witness unto you that Jesus Christ was and is the literal Son of

God and the Savior of all mankind. I promise you that if you want to defy darkness, disappointment, doubt, and the forces of uncertainty that seek to drown you, come to know the Lord, Jesus Christ. To all these philosophical voices I say with the angel who stood at his empty tomb, "Why seek ye the living among the dead?"

Jesus Christ is not just a historical figure. The Christ who was is the Christ who is. He lives today; he is personal; he has a body. His tomb is empty, a symbol for all of us that no darkness — even death — is so deep we cannot overcome it with his help. We can conquer all.

Book designed by Bailey-Montague and Associates
Composed by Column Type
in Palatino with display lines in Avant Garde Medium
Printed by Publishers Press
on 60# Simpson Antique
Bound by Mountain States Bindery